■ はしがき ■

　本書は，第一学習社発行の英語教科書「CREATIVE English Communication II」に完全準拠したワークブックです。各パート見開き2ページで，教科書本文を使って「聞く」「読む」「話す（やり取り）」「話す（発表）」「書く」の4技能5領域の力を育成する問題をバランスよく用意しました。

■ 本書の構成と利用法 ■

各パート，Activity Plus のページ

教科書本文

・新出単語を太字で示しました。

・意味のまとまりごとにスラッシュを入れました。ここで示した意味のまとまりや，英語の強弱のリズム，イントネーションなどに注意して，本文を流暢に音読できるようにしましょう。付属のスピーキング・トレーナーを使って，自分の発話を後から確認できます。発話の流暢さ（1分あたりの発話語数：words per minute）を算出する計算式を，本書巻末にまとめて掲載しています。

📖 Reading

・大学入学共通テストなどの形式に対応した，本文の内容理解問題です。

🔍 Vocabulary & Grammar

・英検®やGTEC®の形式に対応した，新出単語や新出表現，文法事項，重要語句についての問題です。

🎧 Listening

・本文内容やテーマに関連した短い英文を聞いて答える問題です。

・Activity Plus では，本文内容やテーマに関連したやや長い英文を聞いて答える問題を収録しています。

・🔘 は別売の音声CDのトラック番号を示します。二次元コードを読み取って，音声をPCやスマートフォンなどから聞くこともできます。

💬 Interaction

・本文内容やテーマに関連した会話を聞いて，最後の発話に対して自分の考えなどを応答し，やり取りを完成させる活動です。

・付属のスピーキング・トレーナーを使って，自分の発話を後から確認することができます。

💬 Production (Speak)　✏️ Production (Write)

・本文内容やテーマに関連した，自分自身に関する質問や，考えや意見を問う質問に話したり書いたりして答える表現活動です。

◆「知識・技能」や「思考力・判断力・表現力」を養成することを意識し，設問ごとに主に対応する観点を示しました。

◆ライティング，スピーキング問題を自分で採点できるようにしています。

　別冊『解答・解説集』の「ルーブリック評価表」（ある観点における学習の到達度を判断する基準）を用いて，自分の記述内容や発話内容が採点できます。

CONTENTS

CAN-DO List
知識・技能

❏♪さまざまな助動詞, 分詞構文 (現在分詞) や, 語・連語・慣用表現について理解を深め, これらを適切に活用することができる。
❏◀))強弱のリズムを理解して音読することができる。

❏♪受け身の分詞構文, 副詞節中の〈S+be〉の省略や, 語・連語・慣用表現について理解を深め, これらを適切に活用することができる。
❏◀))強弱のリズムを理解して音読することができる。

❏♪関係代名詞の非制限用法, 仮定法過去[過去完了]や, 語・連語・慣用表現について理解を深め, これらを適切に活用することができる。
❏◀))強弱のリズムを理解して音読することができる。

❏♪助動詞+have+過去分詞, 完了不定詞や, 語・連語・慣用表現について理解を深め, これらを適切に活用することができる。
❏◀))イントネーションを理解して音読することができる。

❏♪関係副詞の非制限用法, 同格の that や, 語・連語・慣用表現について理解を深め, これらを適切に活用することができる。
❏◀))イントネーションを理解して音読することができる。

❏♪完了形の分詞構文, 複合関係詞や, 語・連語・慣用表現について理解を深め, これらを適切に活用することができる。
❏◀))イントネーションを理解して音読することができる。

❏♪さまざまな仮定法, 否定語+倒置や, 語・連語・慣用表現について理解を深め, これらを適切に活用することができる。
❏◀))音の変化を理解して音読することができる。

❏♪独立不定詞・独立分詞構文, if... 以外が条件を表す仮定法や, 語・連語・慣用表現について理解を深め, これらを適切に活用することができる。
❏◀))音の変化を理解して音読することができる。

❏♪前置詞+関係代名詞, 強調構文や, 語・連語・慣用表現について理解を深め, これらを適切に活用することができる。
❏◀))音の変化を理解して音読することができる。

❏♪語・連語・慣用表現について理解を深め, これらを適切に活用することができる。
❏◀))シャドーイングをすることができる。

思考力・判断力・表現力

❏📖国連ユース気候サミットの参加者の活動とメッセージについて的確に理解し，その内容を整理することができる。
❏🎧気候変動や環境問題に関する英文を聞いて，必要な情報を把握することができる。
❏💬日常生活について，適切に情報や考えを伝え合うことができる。
❏🗣自分の故郷について，自分の考えを話して伝えることができる。
❏✎環境問題や日常生活について，自分の考えを書いて伝えることができる。

❏📖動物の睡眠について的確に理解し，その内容を整理することができる。
❏🎧動物の生態に関する英文を聞いて，必要な情報を把握することができる。
❏💬動物や自分の睡眠習慣について，適切に情報や考えを伝え合うことができる。
❏🗣好きな動物について，自分の考えを話して伝えることができる。
❏✎健康や睡眠について，情報や考えを書いて伝えることができる。

❏📖アスリートのスピーチに見られる特徴について的確に理解し，その内容を整理することができる。
❏🎧スポーツやスピーチに関する英文を聞いて，必要な情報を把握することができる。
❏💬スポーツやスピーチ，人間関係について，適切に情報や考えを伝え合うことができる。
❏🗣スポーツについて，自分の考えを話して伝えることができる。
❏✎成功，感謝，謙虚さについて，情報や考えを書いて伝えることができる。

❏📖自然災害と防災について的確に理解し，その内容を整理することができる。
❏🎧災害に関する英文を聞いて，必要な情報を把握することができる。
❏💬災害や災害対策について，適切に情報や考えを伝え合うことができる。
❏🗣災害対策について，情報を話して伝えることができる。
❏✎災害対策について，情報や考えを書いて伝えることができる。

❏📖日本および世界の元号について的確に理解し，その内容を整理することができる。
❏🎧元号や歴史に関する英文を聞いて，必要な情報を把握することができる。
❏💬時代や文化，好きな歌詞について，適切に情報や考えを伝え合うことができる。
❏🗣漢字について，自分の考えを話して伝えることができる。
❏✎文化や自分の思い出について，情報や考えを書いて伝えることができる。

❏📖フードロス・フードウェイストの問題について的確に理解し，その内容を整理することができる。
❏🎧食の問題に関する英文を聞いて，必要な情報を把握することができる。
❏💬食生活や食品廃棄について，適切に情報や考えを伝え合うことができる。
❏🗣家庭での食品廃棄について，自分の考えを話して伝えることができる。
❏✎食生活や社会問題について，情報や考えを書いて伝えることができる。

❏📖南谷真鈴さんの冒険と，彼女のメッセージについて的確に理解し，その内容を整理することができる。
❏🎧登山や海外経験，努力や目標に関する英文を聞いて，必要な情報を把握することができる。
❏💬山，経験，将来，目標について，適切に情報や考えを伝え合うことができる。
❏🗣目標について，情報を話して伝えることができる。
❏✎目標や経験，長所と短所について，情報や考えを書いて伝えることができる。

❏📖電池の発展について的確に理解し，その内容を整理することができる。
❏🎧電池・電子機器や科学に関する英文を聞いて，必要な情報を把握することができる。
❏💬日常生活，ノーベル賞について適切に情報や考えを伝え合うことができる。
❏🗣電池を使った製品について，自分の考えを話して伝えることができる。
❏✎日常生活や発明品について，情報や考えを書いて伝えることができる。

❏📖オーバーツーリズムの問題と新しい旅行様式について的確に理解し，その内容を整理することができる。
❏🎧旅行に関する英文を聞いて，必要な情報を把握することができる。
❏💬旅行やその問題点について，適切に情報や考えを伝え合うことができる。
❏🗣観光客と観光地について，自分の考えを話して伝えることができる。
❏✎近年の旅行環境や人助けについて，情報や考えを書いて伝えることができる。

❏📖ストーリーの展開を的確に理解し，その内容を整理することができる。
❏✎日常生活や自分の経験，物語の登場人物の心情について，自分の考えを書いて伝えることができる。

You are learning / about climate change. // On the Internet, / you find an article / about a high school student / who is working / on **environmentally sustainable development**. //

Eva Jones, / an American **female** student / from Hood River Valley High School, / **attended** the United Nations **Youth** Climate **Summit**. // She was one of the 500 young people / selected to join the Summit. // She was also one of the 100 "Green Ticket" winners; / the United Nations Fund / supported her trip / to this event. //

I grew up / in the Columbia Gorge / in the U.S. // There are different communities / and environments there. // I was inspired to be an advocate / for the earth / and the living things / on it. //

I'm **honored** / to be selected / as a voice at the Summit. // Brave action / is the only way / to make a difference / for future generations. // We must have our leaders / take responsibility / seriously. //

We have the power / to stop the bad **effects** / that are changing the earth's climate. // The main way is / to use our money / for encouraging sustainable **consumption** / and for stopping the use / of **unclean** energy. // I'm proud / to **represent** my lovely hometown / and the environmental beauty / I grew up in. //
(192 words)

🔊 音読しよう　　　　　　　　　　　　　　　　　スピーキング・トレーナー
Practice 1　スラッシュ位置で文を区切って読んでみよう☐
Practice 2　英語の強弱のリズムに注意して読んでみよう☐
TRY!　　　　2分以内に本文全体を音読しよう☐

📖 **Reading**　本文の内容を読んで理解しよう【知識・技能】【思考力・判断力・表現力】　　　共通テスト

Make the correct choice to complete each sentence. (各6点)

1. Eva Jones ☐ .

   ① expects future generations to solve the environmental problem

   ② is a high school student who is very interested in climate change problems

   ③ is organizing the United Nations Youth Climate Summit

   ④ says that consumers are responsible for climate change

2. One **fact** stated in the article is that ☐ .

   ① brave action is the only way to solve climate change problems

   ② Columbia Gorge is an environmentally beautiful place

   ③ more than 300 young people attended the United Nations Youth Climate Summit

   ④ we must have leaders who take responsibility

🔍 Vocabulary & Grammar　重要表現や文法事項について理解しよう【知識】　　英検® GTEC®

Make the correct choice to complete each sentence. (各2点)

1.　It is our responsibility to develop environmentally (　　　) products and services.
　　① fixed　　　　　② important　　　　③ sustainable　　　④ unclean

2.　He got into a lot of trouble in his (　　　).
　　① adulthood　　　② child　　　　　　③ honor　　　　　④ youth

3.　These products are not for (　　　) in the country, but for export.
　　① consumable　　② consume　　　　③ consumer　　　④ consumption

4.　Salah was chosen to (　　　) Egypt at the World Cup.
　　① attend　　　　② contribute　　　③ present　　　　④ represent

5.　You (　　　) tell lies that will hurt other people.
　　① can　　　　　② don't have to　　③ must　　　　　④ must not

🎧 Listening　英文を聞いて理解しよう【知識・技能】【思考力・判断力・表現力】　　共通テスト CD 1

Listen to the English and make the best choice to match the content. (4点)

　① The speaker became ill after he attended the lecture.

　② The speaker couldn't make a speech on the environment.

　③ The speaker was going to listen to the lecture.

💬 Interaction　英文を聞いて会話を続けよう【知識・技能】【思考力・判断力・表現力】　スピーキング・トレーナー CD 2

Listen to the English and respond to the last remark. (7点)

　[メ モ　　　　　　　　　　　　　　　　　　　　　　　　　　　　　　　　　　　　]

　アドバイス　単純に質問に答えるだけでなく，その理由などを加えよう。

💬 Production (Speak)　自分の考えを話して伝えよう【思考力・判断力・表現力】　　スピーキング・トレーナー

Speak out your answer to the following question. (7点)

　What is your hometown like?

　アドバイス　本文でエヴァさんが Columbia Gorge について説明しているのを参考に，自分の地元を簡単に描写してみよう。

Climate change / is one of the biggest environmental problems. // These days, / the need to **deal** with it / is becoming **increasingly urgent**. //

① The United Nations Youth Climate Summit / took place / on September 21, / 2019. // It was held / at the UN **Headquarters** / **located** in New York. // Young climate action leaders / presented their ideas / to politicians / all over the world. // The Youth Climate Summit / was followed / by the UN Climate Action Summit / on September 23. //

② Over 7,000 young people / from more than 140 countries and **territories** / **applied** to the Youth Climate Summit. // They were selected / on the basis of how they worked / on climate change / and discussed possible solutions. // Their performances were **evaluated** / by a **panel** / led by UN officials. // After that, / 500 of the young people / were invited to the Summit. // One hundred of them / got "Green Tickets." // These winners received / fully funded travel / to New York. // Their transportation / was as **carbon-neutral** / as possible. // In other words, / they used **vehicles** / which **emitted** less carbon dioxide. //

③ The **participants** shared their ideas / on the global stage. // They delivered / a clear message / to world leaders: / We need to act now / to work / on climate change. // （190 words）

🔊 音読しよう　　　　　　　　　　　　　　　　　　　スピーキング・トレーナー
Practice 1　スラッシュ位置で文を区切って読んでみよう☐
Practice 2　英語の強弱のリズムに注意して読んでみよう☐
TRY!　　　　1分50秒以内に本文全体を音読しよう☐

📖 **Reading**　本文の内容を読んで理解しよう【知識・技能】【思考力・判断力・表現力】　　共通テスト

Make the correct choice to complete each sentence or answer each question. （各4点）

1. How many people attended the United Nations Youth Climate Summit in New York? ☐
   ① 100 people did.　② 140 people did.　③ 500 people did.　④ 7,000 people did.

2. Which of the following is an appropriate example of transportation that is "as carbon-neutral as possible"? ☐
   ① Traveling with the money contributed by the fund.
   ② Traveling in order to participate in environmental events.
   ③ Using a ship powered by wind.
   ④ Using private cars instead of public transportation.

3. The United Nations Youth Climate Summit is [＿＿].

　① a meeting for evaluating young people's efforts to address climate change

　② a meeting for young people to discuss their thoughts on climate change

　③ a meeting for world leaders to determine a clear action plan on climate change

　④ an opportunity for young people to get the "Green ticket"

🔍 Vocabulary & Grammar　重要表現や文法事項について理解しよう【知識】　英検® GTEC®

Make the correct choice to complete each sentence. （各2点）

1. Many people in the world are in (　　　) need of food and water.

　① urgent　　　② every　　　③ little　　　④ various

2. Japanese university students (　　　) to many companies for employment.

　① apply　　　② evaluate　　　③ need　　　④ present

3. The factory (　　　) toxic gas.

　① applies　　　② emits　　　③ holds　　　④ plays

4. Companies must not discriminate on the (　　　) of sex.

　① base　　　② basic　　　③ basics　　　④ basis

5. Information (　　　) by reliable experts and institutions should be given importance.

　① provide　　　② provide to　　　③ provided　　　④ providing

🎧 Listening　英文を聞いて理解しよう【知識・技能】【思考力・判断力・表現力】　共通テスト CD 3

Listen to the English and make the best choice to match the content. （4点）

　① About 400 students were interested in the speech.

　② More than 300 students were not happy with the speech.

　③ Over 300 people didn't want to talk to the president.

💬 Interaction　英文を聞いて会話を続けよう【知識・技能】【思考力・判断力・表現力】　スピーキング・トレーナー CD 4

Listen to the English and respond to the last remark. （7点）

　[メモ　　　　　　　　　　　　　　　　　　　　　　　　　　　　　　　]

　アドバイス　最初の発言は自分の発言です。

✍ Production（Write）　自分の考えを書いて伝えよう【思考力・判断力・表現力】

Write your answer to the following question. （7点）

　What can you do to reduce greenhouse gas emissions?

　アドバイス　温室効果ガスを排出している身近なものを考えてみよう。

----

④ One of the participants / at the Summit / was 15-year-old Aditya Mukarji / from India. // He is working on problems / of plastic pollution. //

⑤ In India, / Aditya helps an NGO / so that businesses can **sort** their waste / and recycle plastics. // He also promotes / the use of more eco-friendly goods / than plastics. // For example, / at the age of 13, / Aditya went to cafés and restaurants, / **persuading** them to use eco-friendly **alternatives** / instead of plastic straws / and other single-use plastics. // He said, / "I'm **hopeful** / about the future / if we can make change / today. // If we wait for another day, / I'm not." // He is promoting / the **philosophy** of "**Refuse** If You Cannot Reuse." //

⑥ Aditya was impressed / by his **fellow attendees** / at the Summit. // "All these youths / who have come here / are excellent in their fields. // They are all the best, / and they are trying / to **empower** other people / to work toward **preventing** climate change," / he said. // "They all have the same ideal: / to save the earth. // They all have / different approaches." // (165 words)

🔊 音読しよう　　　　　　　　　　　　　　　　スピーキング・トレーナー
Practice 1　スラッシュ位置で文を区切って読んでみよう☐
Practice 2　英語の強弱のリズムに注意して読んでみよう☐
TRY!　　　　1分40秒以内に本文全体を音読しよう☐

📖 **Reading**　本文の内容を読んで理解しよう【知識・技能】【思考力・判断力・表現力】　共通テスト

Make the correct choice to complete each sentence. (1. 完答 8 点, 2. 4 点)

1. Aditya Mukarji is working on environmental problems, especially ☐A☐ problems. He encourages businesses to use ☐B☐ materials other than the conventional ones which cannot be reused.

　① eco-friendly　　② plastic waste　　③ single-use　　④ plastic straws

2. One **fact** stated by Aditya is that ☐　☐.
　① all the attendees at the summit are excellent
　② each participant in the summit has a different approach
　③ the sooner we make a change, the better
　④ we should refuse items that we cannot reuse

6

🔊 英語の強弱のリズムを理解して音読することができる。　　📖 環境活動に関する英文を読んで，概要や要点を捉えることができる。
🔍 文脈を理解して適切な語句を用いて英文を完成することができる。　🎧 平易な英語で話される短い英文を聞いて必要な情報を聞き取ることができる。
✏️ 紙製品について簡単な語句を用いて説明することができる。　　✍️ プラスチック代替製品について簡単な語句を用いて考えを表現することができる。

oals

🔍 Vocabulary & Grammar　重要表現や文法事項について理解しよう【知識】　英検® GTEC®

Make the correct choice to complete each sentence. (各2点)

1. He is trying to repair the machine so (　　　) it works properly.

　① as　　　　　　　② for　　　　　　　③ that　　　　　　④ to

2. She (　　　) her friend to go back home because he looked sick.

　① persuaded　　　② sorted　　　　　③ promoted　　　　④ waited

3. They asked her to throw away the garbage, but she (　　　).

　① recycled　　　　② reduced　　　　　③ refused　　　　　④ reused

4. Fasten your seatbelt to (　　　) serious injury.

　① help　　　　　　② intend　　　　　　③ prevent　　　　　④ stop

5. (　　　) the news, I was so surprised that I couldn't speak.

　① Hear　　　　　　② Heard　　　　　　③ Hearing　　　　　④ To hearing

🎧 Listening　英文を聞いて理解しよう【知識・技能】【思考力・判断力・表現力】　共通テスト　CD 5

Listen to the English and make the best choice to match the content. (4点)

① The speaker doesn't need any plastic bag.

② The speaker doesn't want bigger plastic bags.

③ The speaker will have two different sizes of bags.

💬 Interaction　英文を聞いて会話を続けよう【知識・技能】【思考力・判断力・表現力】　スピーキング・トレーナー　CD 6

Listen to the English and respond to the last remark. (7点)

［メモ　　　］

　アドバイス　そのとき感じたことなど，会話を広げる補足情報を加えよう。

✏️ Production (Write)　自分の考えを書いて伝えよう【思考力・判断力・表現力】

Write your answer to the following question. (7点)

　Do you use any eco-friendly alternatives instead of plastic products? What are they?

　アドバイス　まずは身近な使い捨てプラスチックの製品を挙げて，それを何で代替できるか考えてみよう。

⑦ Fifteen-year-old Lesein Mathenge Mutunkei / from **Kenya** / also joined the Summit. // He **belonged** to a soccer team / and began his "Trees4Goals" activity / in 2018. // "I used to plant one tree / for every goal / I scored. // But now / I plant 11 trees / for every goal," / said Lesein. // He has planted / more than 1,400 trees. // He also keeps track of the places / where he planted the trees / so that he can make sure / that they are growing. //

⑧ Lesein respects Wangari Maathai, / a **Kenyan** environmental **activist**. // She took the **initiative** / in planting trees / in Africa. // He always keeps her words / in mind: / "I will be / a **hummingbird**; / I will do / the best I can." // In an **Ecuadorean** folk **tale**, / only the little hummingbird / tried to protect the forest / from a big fire. //

⑨ Lesein wants to learn / new ways / to help save the planet. // "Maathai did her part, / and now / it is time / for young people / to do their part. // Any little thing we do / can be a help. // Planting a tree, / picking up **litter**, / or even sharing information / on the Internet / ... everything counts," / he says. // (182 words)

◀)) 音読しよう   スピーキング・トレーナー
Practice 1 スラッシュ位置で文を区切って読んでみよう ☐
Practice 2 英語の強弱のリズムに注意して読んでみよう ☐
TRY!   １分50秒以内に本文全体を音読しよう ☐

📖 **Reading** 本文の内容を読んで理解しよう【知識・技能】【思考力・判断力・表現力】   共通テスト

Make the correct choice to complete each sentence or answer each question. (各4点)

1. Lesein Mathenge Mutunkei ☐ .
   ① has scored more than 100 goals since he started "Trees4Goals"
   ② is a soccer player who plants trees for each game he plays
   ③ joined the soccer team to work on environmental issues after attending the summit
   ④ not only plants trees but he grows them himself

2. What did Maathai probably feel when she said, "I'll be a hummingbird"? ☐
   ① She felt it was more important for her to tackle the problem earlier than anyone else, rather than whether she could solve it or not.
   ② She felt she was not powerful, but she wanted to do something to solve a big problem.
   ③ She wanted to go into the Ecuadorean folk tale and prevent the forest fire.
   ④ She felt the problem was beyond her abilities to solve on her own.

3. Lesein says ☐ to save the planet.

   ① everyone should plant trees

   ② only picking up litter is not enough

   ③ using Internet can be a new way

   ④ young people should do something, even if it's a small thing,

🔍 Vocabulary & Grammar　重要表現や文法事項について理解しよう【知識】　　英検® GTEC®

Make the correct choice to complete each sentence. (各 2 点)

1. Who does this watch (　　　) to?

   ① belong　　　　② function　　　　③ have　　　　④ work

2. Ken is showing (　　　) on the job and will be soon promoted.

   ① arrogance　　　② initiative　　　③ laziness　　　④ performance

3. Are you telling (　　　)? Please tell the truth.

   ① differences　　② dreams　　　　③ secrets　　　④ tales

4. Most of the packaging we often see in our daily life ends up as (　　　).

   ① energy　　　　② litter　　　　　③ material　　　④ pollution

5. I (　　　) soccer after school.

   ① use to play　　② use to playing　　③ used to play　　④ used to playing

🎧 Listening　英文を聞いて理解しよう【知識・技能】【思考力・判断力・表現力】　　共通テスト 💿⁷

Listen to the English and make the best choice to match the content. (4 点)

   ① Bill told the speaker to do something for the environment.

   ② The speaker decided to plant trees.

   ③ The speaker gave some advice to Bill.

💬 Interaction　英文を聞いて会話を続けよう【知識・技能】【思考力・判断力・表現力】　スピーキング・トレーナー 💿⁸

Listen to the English and respond to the last remark. (7 点)

   [メモ　　　　　　　　　　　　　　　　　　　　　　　　　　　　　　　　]

   アドバイス 質問に対する「はい」か「いいえ」の返答を忘れないようにしよう。

✍ Production（Write）　自分の考えを書いて伝えよう【思考力・判断力・表現力】

Write your answer to the following question. (7 点)

   Do you have a social media account? What do you use it for?

   アドバイス social media とは，twitter や Instagram などの SNS のことです。

In an English class, / a teacher and three students are speaking / at a **mock** youth climate summit. / You are listening / to them. //

Teacher: Here / we have three excellent climate activists. // Now, / please share your actions / for protecting the environment. // Will you start, / Kazuki? //

Kazuki: Well, / I'm interested / in engineering. // I read a book / about an African boy / who made a **windmill** / that **generates** electricity. // We need / **renewable** energy sources / to replace **generators** / which use fossil fuels. //

Teacher: So, / Kazuki, / you believe / that we must replace fossil fuels / with more eco-friendly energy sources. // Next, / can you tell us / what you're doing, / Emily? //

Emily: I'm planning / to write a letter / to **convince** our school's **administration** / to install solar panels. // I started looking for **supporters** / and have found teachers and friends / who agree with my idea. // The more supporters I have, / the stronger my **appeal** will become. //

Teacher: Thank you, / Emily! // You're saying / that finding more supporters for your idea / is the key. // Satoshi, / how about you? // What action / are you taking? //

Satoshi: I started studying **economics** / as well as environmental **issues**. // Some world leaders are saying / that young activists should calm down / and study economics first. // If I have some **knowledge** / about economics, / my ideas about environmental issues / will be more convincing. //

Teacher: I see, / Satoshi. // Your point is / that it is important / to make your opinion **persuasive**. // (219 words)

🔊 音読しよう　　　　　　　　　　　　　　　　　　　スピーキング・トレーナー

Practice 1　スラッシュ位置で文を区切って読んでみよう ☐
Practice 2　英語の強弱のリズムに注意して読んでみよう ☐
TRY!　　　　2分10秒以内に本文全体を音読しよう ☐

📖 **Reading**　本文の内容を読んで理解しよう【知識・技能】【思考力・判断力・表現力】　共通テスト

Make the correct choice to complete each sentence or answer each question. (各6点)

1. Two of the three students are talking about ☐.

① clean energy　　② economy　　③ engineering　　④ supporters

2. Satoshi ☐.

① is studying economics because he wants to have convincing ideas

② studies economics first to calm down

③ believes economy is more important than the environmental issues

④ thinks world leaders aren't working on environmental issues in order to sustain their economies

🔍 Vocabulary & Grammar　重要表現や文法事項について理解しよう【知識】　英検® GTEC®

Make the correct choice to complete each sentence. (各2点)

1. In that country, windmills are used to (　　　) electricity.
   ① consume　　　② expect　　　③ generate　　　④ proceed

2. I tried to (　　　) myself that I was doing the right thing.
   ① convince　　　② decide　　　③ forgive　　　④ manage

3. In his speech, he referred to various social (　　　) of our time, from environmental problems to inequality between the rich and poor.
   ① issues　　　② distances　　　③ behaviors　　　④ gaps

4. Since she worked in the publishing industry, she has learned much (　　　) about copyright.
   ① knowledge　　　② process　　　③ tolerance　　　④ strictness

5. Can you replace the light bulb in the bathroom (　　　) a new one?
   ① at　　　② for　　　③ to　　　④ with

6. You (　　　) tell this story to anyone else. It's an absolute secret.
   ① don't have to　　　② had better not　　　③ had not better　　　④ have to

7. She's angry with you. You (　　　) apologize.
   ① can　　　② ought to　　　③ used to　　　④ would

8. (　　　) nothing to do, he spent the whole day reading.
   ① Had　　　② Have　　　③ Having　　　④ To have

🎧 Listening　英文を聞いて理解しよう【知識・技能】【思考力・判断力・表現力】　共通テスト　CD 9

Listen to the English and make the best choice to match the content. (4点)

1. Where did Greta come from to New York?
   ① Sweden　　　　　② The United Nations
   ③ The U.K.　　　　④ The U.S.

2. How long did it take for Greta to travel to the U.S?
   ① For about two weeks.　　　② For fifteen weeks.
   ③ For seventeen days.　　　　④ For sixty days.

3. Which of the following is true about Greta's speech?
   ① Greta thanked world leaders for their support.
   ② Scientists moved to New York to listen to her speech.
   ③ She gave the speech on the 23rd of October.
   ④ She talked for several minutes at the summit.

You and your friend / are visiting a zoo. // At the entrance, / you are given / a picture card / which shows the **lifestyles** / of three animals. // On the card, / each animal asks you / to guess what animal / it is. //

Who Am I? //

The answer to each "Who Am I?" question is / in front of our cages. //

Please come and see us! //

Animal No.1 //

I almost always live / in a tree / and **seldom descend** / to the ground. // I only eat / the leaves of a specific tree, / and I usually don't drink / water. // I don't like moving around, / but I like sleeping / very much. // I sleep / about 20 hours / a day. // Who am I? //

Animal No.2 //

I am very tall, / and I like eating the leaves / of tall trees. // I have to eat / a large amount of leaves / every day. // My **tongue** can **extend** / up to 50 centimeters / out of my mouth, / so I can take many leaves / off a **branch** / at a time. // I only sleep / about two hours / a day / because I am busy eating. // Who am I? //

Animal No.3 //

The **rainforest** is my home / and I never go down / to the ground. // I don't have a family, / and I live / all by myself. // I have long arms / that are about twice as long / as my legs. // My favorite food / is fruit. // I make a bed / to sleep in / with branches I take / from trees. // Who am I? // (236 words)

🔊 **音読しよう**

スピーキング・トレーナー

Practice 1	スラッシュ位置で文を区切って読んでみよう ☐
Practice 2	英語の強弱のリズムに注意して読んでみよう ☐
TRY!	2分20秒以内に本文全体を音読しよう ☐

📖 **Reading**　本文の内容を読んで理解しよう【知識・技能】【思考力・判断力・表現力】　共通テスト

Make the correct choice to complete each sentence or answer each question. (各4点)

1. Animal No.1 ☐ .

   ① doesn't like sleeping

   ② only eats meat

   ③ seldom climbs a tree

   ④ usually doesn't drink water

2. Which of the following is true about Animal No.2? ☐

   ① It is very tall and likes eating meat.

   ② It is very tall and sleeps about 20 hours a day.

   ③ Its tongue is very long and it eats a lot of leaves.

   ④ Its tongue is very long and it sleeps about 20 hours a day.

3. Which of the following is **not** true about Animal No.3? ☐

　① It can make a bed with branches.

　② It has a big family and lives with them.

　③ It has long arms and likes fruit.

　④ It lives in the rainforest and always stays in trees.

🔍 **Vocabulary & Grammar**　　重要表現や文法事項について理解しよう【知識】　　英検® GTEC®

Make the correct choice to complete each sentence. (各2点)

1. Sally was busy (　　　) a report last night.

　① have made　　　② made　　　③ make　　　④ making

2. I pushed the button and waited for the elevator to (　　　).

　① decrease　　　② descend　　　③ fall　　　④ step

3. Did you check the latest lottery? We can win (　　　) $10,000 in this lottery.

　① up to　　　② up and down　　　③ up over　　　④ up with

4. They need to (　　　) their stay from five days to ten days.

　① extend　　　② long　　　③ stretch　　　④ spread

5. (　　　) hungry, she dropped in at McDonald's.

　① Being　　　② Having　　　③ Since he is　　　④ To be

🎧 **Listening**　　英文を聞いて理解しよう【知識・技能】【思考力・判断力・表現力】　　共通テスト CD 10

Listen to the English and make the best choice to match the content. (4点)

　① Adult dogs usually sleep for more than half a day.

　② Dogs get up later than humans in the morning.

　③ Young dogs don't sleep longer than adult dogs.

💬 **Interaction**　　英文を聞いて会話を続けよう【知識・技能】【思考力・判断力・表現力】　スピーキング・トレーナー　CD 11

Listen to the English and respond to the last remark. (7点)

　［メモ　　］

　　アドバイス　相手が知りたいことは何かを考えよう。「いいえ」の場合は質問し返したり，予想を答えたりして対話
　　　　　　　を続けよう。

💬 **Production（Speak）**　　自分の考えを話して伝えよう【思考力・判断力・表現力】　　スピーキング・トレーナー

Speak out your answer to the following question. (7点)

　　Have you ever been to the zoo? What animal do you like to see?

　　アドバイス　理由などを忘れずに付け加えよう。

13

How long do animals sleep? // Do most animals sleep / as long as human beings do / every day? //

① In **general**, / human beings need / seven to eight hours of sleep / every night / in order to stay healthy. // This means / that we spend / about one third of our whole life / sleeping. // However, / what about other animals? // Sleeping time **varies** / greatly / from animal to animal. // For **instance**, / koalas sleep / for about 20 hours / a day, / but giraffes' sleeping time / is amazingly short /——only about two hours / a day. //

② Koalas **mostly** live / in trees, / and they feed, / sleep or rest / most of the time. // They eat / only **eucalyptus** leaves. // The leaves have / a high water **content** / but are poor / in **nutrition**. // **Therefore**, / koalas don't get / enough energy / from their **diet** / to move around much. //

③ Eucalyptus leaves / also contain **toxins** / that are hard / for other animals / to remove. // Koalas can get **rid** of / these toxins, / but it takes a lot of energy / to do that. // It is thought / that they save energy / by doing nothing / **besides** eating / and resting. // (174 words)

🔊 音読しよう

スピーキング・トレーナー

Practice 1　スラッシュ位置で文を区切って読んでみよう ☐
Practice 2　英語の強弱のリズムに注意して読んでみよう ☐
TRY!　　　1分40秒以内に本文全体を音読しよう ☐

📖 **Reading**　本文の内容を読んで理解しよう【知識・技能】【思考力・判断力・表現力】　　共通テスト

Make the correct choice to complete each sentence or answer each question. (各4点)

1. Human beings spend about ☐ .

   ① 20% of our whole life sleeping

   ② 33% of our whole life sleeping

   ③ one fourth of our whole life sleeping

   ④ two thirds of our whole life sleeping

2. Which of the following is true about koalas' food? ☐

   ① They don't have to eat nutritious foods because they don't move around much.

   ② They eat only eucalyptus leaves because they are rich in nutrition.

   ③ They eat only eucalyptus leaves but the leaves are low in nutrition.

   ④ They eat various leaves which have a high water content.

3. Which of the following is true about koalas' special ability? ☐

   ① They can create toxins that other animals can't remove.

   ② They can get enough energy from their food to move around.

   ③ They can get rid of the toxins of eucalyptus leaves.

   ④ They can remove the toxins with little energy consumption.

🔍 Vocabulary & Grammar 　重要表現や文法事項について理解しよう【知識】 　英検® GTEC®

Make the correct choice to complete each sentence. (各2点)

1. It is not easy for her family to (　　　) a lot of old vases which her grandfather collected.

① get along 　　② get on 　　③ get up 　　④ get rid of

2. The former president improved the (　　) of the children.

① nutrition 　　② nutritional 　　③ nutritionally 　　④ nutritious

3. Tom gave a presentation about new bacteria (　　).

① dangerous 　　② harmless 　　③ toxins 　　④ toxic

4. Unfortunately, Anna doesn't trust anyone (　　) herself.

① along 　　② besides 　　③ through 　　④ within

5. The laundry will not dry quickly (　) it's sunny.

① because 　　② if 　　③ unless 　　④ whether

🎧 Listening 　英文を聞いて理解しよう【知識・技能】【思考力・判断力・表現力】 　共通テスト CD 12

Listen to the English and make the best choice to match the content. (4点)

① Adult koalas don't usually give food to baby koalas.

② Baby koalas don't eat the same food as adult koalas.

③ Baby koalas easily remove the toxins of eucalyptus leaves by themselves.

💬 Interaction 　英文を聞いて会話を続けよう【知識・技能】【思考力・判断力・表現力】 　スピーキング・トレーナー CD 13

Listen to the English and respond to the last remark. (7点)

[メモ　　　　　　　　　　　　　　　　　　　　　　　　　　　　　　]

アドバイス 　自分はどうか，考えてみよう。

✐ Production (Write) 　自分の考えを書いて伝えよう【思考力・判断力・表現力】

Write your answer to the following question. (7点)

What do you usually do to stay healthy?

アドバイス 　とくにしていることがない場合でも，その理由などを述べよう。

----

④　In **contrast** to koalas, / giraffes sleep / only for short periods of time. // **Modern** research shows / that giraffes usually sleep / only about two hours / a day / in total. // They mostly stand / while sleeping, / and they lie down / on the ground / to sleep / for only a few minutes. // Giraffes are the tallest land animals, / and they need to eat / a huge amount of leaves / every day / to **maintain** / their large bodies. // They have to spend / far more time feeding / than sleeping. //

⑤　Most large **grazing mammals**, / such as giraffes, / horses / and elephants, / are short-**sleepers**. // It takes many hours / for these animals / to eat a lot of leaves / or grass. // It is thought / that they evolved into short-sleepers / because they needed / to reduce the danger / of being attacked / by **predators** / like lions, / **leopards** / and **hyenas**. //

⑥　Meat-eating animals, / on the other hand, / sleep as much as / 13 to 15 hours / a day. // Their food contains / lots of **protein**, / so / it is very **nutritious**. // Therefore, / they don't have to spend / a great amount of time / feeding. //

(170 words)

🔊 **音読しよう**

Practice 1　スラッシュ位置で文を区切って読んでみよう □
Practice 2　英語の強弱のリズムに注意して読んでみよう □
TRY!　　　　1分40秒以内に本文全体を音読しよう □

スピーキング・トレーナー

📖 **Reading**　本文の内容を読んで理解しよう【知識・技能】【思考力・判断力・表現力】　共通テスト

Make the correct choice to complete each sentence or answer each question. (各4点)

1.　How do giraffes sleep? ☐

　① They rarely sleeps while they are standing.

　② They sleep standing up and never lie down on the ground.

　③ They usually stand most of the time they are asleep.

　④ They usually lie down on the ground and sleep for two hours.

2.　Which of the following animals probably sleeps the least? ☐

　① cow　　　　　② dog　　　　　③ mouse　　　　　④ tiger

3.　☐ A ☐ need to reduce the danger of being attacked by ☐ B ☐.

　① A: Grazing mammals　　B: birds

　② A: Grazing mammals　　B: predators

　③ A: Predators　　B: grazing mammals

　④ A: Predators　　B: lizards

英語の強弱のリズムを理解して音読することができる。
草食［肉食］動物の睡眠に関する英文を読んで，概要や要点を捉えることができる。
文脈を理解して適切な語句を用いて英文を完成することができる。
平易な英語で話される短い英文を聞いて必要な情報を聞き取ることができる。　　睡眠習慣について簡単な語句を用いて説明することができる。
自分が朝型か夜型かについて簡単な語句を用いて考えを表現することができる。

oals

🔍 Vocabulary & Grammar   重要表現や文法事項について理解しよう【知識】   英検。 GTEC。

Make the correct choice to complete each sentence.（各2点）

1. It costs the city one million dollars to (　　　) the ancient ruins.
   ① main　　　　　② mainly　　　　　③ maintain　　　　④ maintenance

2. ABC Corporation has (　　　) a top company in this city.
   ① evolved in　　② evolved into　　③ revolved in　　④ revolved into

3. You must pay 10,000 yen (　　　) for dinner. The restaurant is not reasonable.
   ① highly　　　　② in total　　　　　③ more than　　　　④ together

4. (　　　) to his appearance, he was kind and friendly.
   ① In contrast　　② In effect　　　　③ In favor　　　　④ In turn

5. They were close friends (　　　) in junior high school.
   ① they　　　　　② when　　　　　　③ when he　　　　④ when they

🎧 Listening   英文を聞いて理解しよう【知識・技能】【思考力・判断力・表現力】   共通テスト CD 14

Listen to the English and make the best choice to match the content.（4点）

① The giraffe looks at its back when it sleeps.

② The giraffe sleeps with its face on the ground.

③ The giraffe's face is on its body.

💬 Interaction   英文を聞いて会話を続けよう【知識・技能】【思考力・判断力・表現力】   スピーキング・トレーナー   CD 15

Listen to the English and respond to the last remark.（7点）

［メモ　　　　　　　　　　　　　　　　　　　　　　　　　　　　　　　　　　　　　　　］

アドバイス 自分の生活をふり返ってみよう。

✏️ Production（Write）   自分の考えを書いて伝えよう【思考力・判断力・表現力】

Write your answer to the following question.（7点）

Are you an early bird or a night owl?

アドバイス an early bird「朝型人間」, a night owl「夜型人間」

⑦ Some **marine** mammals, / such as whales and dolphins, / have different sleeping styles. // They have to come **regularly** / up to the surface / of the sea / to **breathe**. // It is **impossible** / for them / to sleep / with both their brains and their bodies resting / **entirely**. // They have to keep / swimming and breathing / while sleeping. //

⑧ Dolphins are unique / in that / they keep one brain **hemisphere** / in slow-wave activity / while they sleep. // During slow-wave activity, / the hemispheres of a dolphin's brain / sleep **alternately**, / and they each sleep / for only a short time. // The left hemisphere / is sleeping / while the right eye is closed. // **Similarly**, / the right hemisphere / is **inactive** / while the left eye is closed. // The dolphins repeat this **behavior** / **countless** times / while they are sleeping. //

⑨ **Affected** by their living environments, / all animals / on the **globe** / have developed / different sleep behaviors / and different sleeping hours. // Their lifestyles are / the results of evolution / and **specialization**. // Research on animal sleep / has made many interesting facts / clear to us. // (161 words)

🔊 **音読しよう**   スピーキング・トレーナー
Practice 1   スラッシュ位置で文を区切って読んでみよう ☐
Practice 2   英語の強弱のリズムに注意して読んでみよう ☐
TRY!   1分40秒以内に本文全体を音読しよう ☐

📖 **Reading**   本文の内容を読んで理解しよう【知識・技能】【思考力・判断力・表現力】   共通テスト

Make the correct choice to complete each sentence or answer each question. (各4点)

1. Marine mammals, such as whales and dolphins, ☐.

   ① can sleep for a long period of time without breathing

   ② can swim and breathe while they are sleeping

   ③ don't need to breathe for a long period of time

   ④ never sleep because they have to come up to the surface of the sea to breathe

2. Which of the following is true about dolphins' sleep behavior? ☐

   ① Both right and left brains sleep at the same time.

   ② One of the brain hemispheres seldom becomes inactive while sleeping.

   ③ The right and left brains sleep alternately when they sleep.

   ④ While the left eye is closed, the left hemisphere is sleeping.

3. All animals have evolved their sleep behaviors ☐.

   ① based on their environment

   ② in order to be protected by humans

   ③ instead of changing their lifestyles

   ④ though they didn't want to do so

🔊 英語の強弱のリズムを理解して音読することができる。　　　　　📖 半球睡眠に関する英文を読んで，概要や要点を捉えることができる。
🔍 文脈を理解して適切な語句を用いて英文を完成することができる。
🎧 平易な英語で話される短い英文を聞いて必要な情報を聞き取ることができる。
💬 睡眠習慣について簡単な語句を用いて説明することができる。
✏️ よく眠れるときについて簡単な語句を用いて考えを表現することができる。

oals

🔍 Vocabulary & Grammar　重要表現や文法事項について理解しよう【知識】　　　英検 ® | GTEC ®

Make the correct choice to complete each sentence. (各2点)

1. Do you think that this decision (　　　) them?

① acts　　　　　② affects　　　　　③ arrests　　　　　④ attacks

2. It was (　　　) for us to swim in the sea.　Some sharks had been seen around there.

① able　　　　　② cannot　　　　　③ impossible　　　　　④ permit

3. Our teacher was angry with us and he told us to think about good (　　　) more.

① beauty　　　　② become　　　　③ behavior　　　　④ behind

4. Before giving a speech, (　　　) deeply.

① blank　　　　　② break　　　　　③ breath　　　　　④ breathe

5. (　　　) all over the world, the song is the singer's greatest work.

① Being loving　　② Love　　　　　③ Loved　　　　　④ Loving

🎧 Listening　英文を聞いて理解しよう【知識・技能】【思考力・判断力・表現力】　共通テスト CD 16

Listen to the English and make the best choice to match the content. (4点)

① Satoshi could swim as well as dolphins.

② The speaker heard about dolphins.

③ The speaker wants to swim with dolphins.

💬 Interaction　英文を聞いて会話を続けよう【知識・技能】【思考力・判断力・表現力】　スピーキング・トレーナー CD 17

Listen to the English and respond to the last remark. (7点)

[メモ　　　　　　　　　　　　　　　　　　　　　　　　　　　　　　　　　　　　　　]

アドバイス　どちらを使っているかに加えて，もう片方とどう違うのか自分の意見を述べられるとよいでしょう。

✏️ Production (Write)　自分の考えを書いて伝えよう【思考力・判断力・表現力】

Write your answer to the following question. (7点)

What makes you sleep well?

アドバイス　よく眠れたときはどんな状況だったか考えてみよう。また，よく眠るために何をしているかを考えてもよいでしょう。

A Japanese high school student asks some questions / of an **expert** / who studies human sleep. // The expert answers the student, / showing graphs. //

Student: Do you think / Japanese people **generally** get / enough sleep? //

Expert: According to a **recent** survey, / the **average** sleeping time / of Japanese adults / is getting shorter. // As Graph 1 shows, / the number of people / who sleep less than six hours / every day / has been increasing, / and the number of people / getting more than seven hours of sleep / has been decreasing. //

Student: What's the purpose of sleep? // What is important / about sleep? //

Expert: Sleep helps us / get rid of our **fatigue**. // It is also important / for **refreshing** our brain / and keeping it healthy. // A **shortage** of sleep is bad / for our health, / and it increases / our risk of **obesity** / and heart disease. // Eventually, / it raises our risk of death. //

Student: Is it better / for us / to sleep as long as we can / to stay healthy? //

Expert: Sleeping too long / may not be better / for us. // One interesting fact / we have learned from studies is / that those who sleep longer / than eight hours / a day / have a higher risk of death, / too, / like short-sleepers. // Graph 2 shows / that people who sleep / around seven hours / a day / have the lowest risk of death. // (206 words)

🔊 **音読しよう**　　　　　　　　　　　　　　　　　　スピーキング・トレーナー
Practice 1　スラッシュ位置で文を区切って読んでみよう ☐
Practice 2　英語の強弱のリズムに注意して読んでみよう ☐
TRY!　　　2分以内に本文全体を音読しよう ☐

📖 **Reading**　本文の内容を読んで理解しよう【知識・技能】【思考力・判断力・表現力】　　　共通テスト

Make the correct choice to complete each sentence or answer each question.

(1. 4点, 2. 完答8点)

1. Which of the following is true? ☐

   ① A shortage of sleep has turned out to be better for the health than too much sleep.

   ② A shortage of sleep might cause serious disease and increase the risk of death.

   ③ Short-sleepers can remove more fatigue than long-sleepers.

   ④ The people who sleep more than ten hours don't have risk of death.

2. The people who sleep ☐A☐ have the lowest risk of death but the people who sleep ☐B☐ and ☐C☐ have a higher risk of death.

   ① around seven hours a day　　　　② less than eight hours a day

   ③ longer than eight hours a day　　④ short-sleepers

🔍 Vocabulary & Grammar　重要表現や文法事項について理解しよう【知識】　英検® GTEC®

Make the correct choice to complete each sentence. (各2点)

1. Karen is (　　　) in teaching English for children.
   ① an expert　　　② an example　　　③ an export　　　④ an excuse

2. It has been rainy in (　　　) days.
   ① recent　　　② recently　　　③ regular　　　④ regularly

3. The bad weather caused a food (　　　) in the country.
   ① short　　　② shortage　　　③ shorten　　　④ shortly

4. Write your idea in (　　　) 150 words in English.
   ① least　　　② less than　　　③ no more　　　④ than

5. He (　　　) a complicated question (　　　) a lawyer and was given helpful advice.
   ① asked / in　　　② asked / of　　　③ said / to　　　④ talked / of

6. (　　　) pink, the building stands out in this area.
   ① Have painting　　② Paint　　③ Painted　　④ Painting

7. If (　　　) in the freezer, the ice cream will not melt.
   ① have kept　　② it will keep　　③ keep　　④ kept

8. I would like you to check my report if (　　　).
   ① any　　　② not　　　③ possible　　　④ so

🎧 Listening　英文を聞いて理解しよう【知識・技能】【思考力・判断力・表現力】　共通テスト　CD 18

Listen to the English and make the best choice to match the content. (各4点)

1. According to the speaker, which animals are winter sleepers?
   ① Bears.　　② Insects.　　③ Mice.　　④ Snakes.

2. Why do some small mammals sleep all through the winter?
   ① Because it's too cold for them to move around.
   ② Because their body temperature drops to nearly zero degrees Celsius.
   ③ Because they can't get what they eat.
   ④ Because they must protect themselves from their enemies.

3. Which of the following is true about the speech?
   ① All small animals sleep during the winter without waking up.
   ② Animals sleep in winter because they can't catch other animals.
   ③ Some animals eat a lot of food before winter sleep.
   ④ Some mammals eat their fat when they wake up from winter sleep.

You found / two short video **clips** / of tennis player / Naomi Osaka's **victory** speeches / on the Internet. // You are watching them. //

A: Naomi's speech / after her final match / against Serena Williams / (USA) / in the 2018 U.S. Open Championships //

I know / that everyone was cheering / for Serena Williams, / and I'm sorry / our final match / had to end / like this. // I'd just like to / thank all of you / for coming / and watching / this match. //

It was always my dream / to play with Serena / in the U.S. Open finals. // So / I'm glad / that I was able to / do that, / and I'm **grateful** / I was able to / play with her. // Thank you! //

B: Naomi's speech / after her final match / against Petra Kvitová / (the **Czech Republic**) / in the 2019 Australian Open Championships //

Huge **congrats** / to you, / Petra, / and your team! // I've always wanted / to play with you. // And you've been through / hardships. // You're really amazing. // I was honored / to play with you / in the final. //

Even though it's very hot, / many people still came / to show support, / so I want / to show my **gratitude** / to them, / too. // So, / thanks to Craig, / the tournament director, / the ball kids / running around / in the heat, / the **umpires**, / the volunteers, / everyone. // They make this tournament possible, / so I want / to thank them all, / too. // And thanks / to my team. // There is always a team / behind a tennis player. //　(228 words)

🔊 音読しよう　　　　　　　　　　　　　　　　　スピーキング・トレーナー

Practice 1　スラッシュ位置で文を区切って読んでみよう☐
Practice 2　英語の強弱のリズムに注意して読んでみよう☐
TRY!　　　2分20秒以内に本文全体を音読しよう☐

📖 **Reading**　本文の内容を読んで理解しよう【知識・技能】【思考力・判断力・表現力】　　共通テスト

Make the correct choice to complete each sentence or answer each question. (各6点)

1. In speech A, Naomi says she is glad because ☐.

① her apology was accepted

② her dream came true

③ she played better than Serena

④ she was cheered for by many people

🔊 英語の強弱のリズムを理解して音読することができる。　　　　　📖 大坂なおみ選手のスピーチを読んで，概要や要点を捉えることができる。
🔍 文脈を理解して適切な語句を用いて英文を完成することができる。
🎧 平易な英語で話される短い英文を聞いて必要な情報を聞き取ることができる。
💬 スピーチのトピックについて簡単な語句を用いて考えを表現することができる。
💬 スピーチについて簡単な語句を用いて考えを表現することができる。
oals

2. Which of the following is true about Petra Kvitová? ☐

① Her job is to pick up balls in the court and pass them to the players.

② She defeated Naomi Osaka in the 2019 Australian Open Championships.

③ She thanked all the people who were involved in the tournament.

④ She was praised by Naomi Osaka for overcoming her hardships.

🔍 Vocabulary & Grammar　重要表現や文法事項について理解しよう【知識】　英検® GTEC®

Make the correct choice to complete each sentence. (各2点)

1. His goal led his team to (　　　) in the game.

① agreement　　② frustration　　③ passion　　④ victory

2. I'm (　　　) for the support I have received from my friends and teachers in this school.

① apologize　　② appreciate　　③ cheering　　④ grateful

3. Let me express my sincere (　　　) for all your help.

① attitude　　② congratulations　　③ gratitude　　④ kindness

4. Don't give up! I am always cheering (　　　) you.

① at　　② for　　③ up　　④ with

5. I like people (　　　) have their own ideas.

① what　　② which　　③ who　　④ whom

🎧 Listening　英文を聞いて理解しよう【知識・技能】【思考力・判断力・表現力】　共通テスト CD 19

Listen to the English and make the best choice to match the content. (4点)

① Naomi didn't make a speech.

② The speaker didn't look for the video on the Internet.

③ The speaker probably could enjoy the speech.

💬 Interaction　英文を聞いて会話を続けよう【知識・技能】【思考力・判断力・表現力】　スピーキング・トレーナー CD 20

Listen to the English and respond to the last remark. (7点)

[メモ　　　　　　　　　　　　　　　　　　　　　　　　　　　　　　　]

アドバイス　最初の発言はあなたの発言です。次の発言で何を聞かれているかを注意して聞き取ろう。

💬 Production (Speak)　自分の考えを話して伝えよう【思考力・判断力・表現力】　スピーキング・トレーナー

Speak out your answer to the following question. (7点)

Do you like giving speeches in front of the public? Why or why not?

アドバイス　理由を付け加えるのを忘れないようにしよう。

Professional athletes / around the world / often make a victory speech / in English. // Their speeches have / some features / in common. // What are they? //

① What do athletes tell people / in their victory speeches / after the competition is over? // You can find / four features / in their speeches / that **attract** people. // They are: / to honor their **opponents**, / to **acknowledge** their opponents' achievements, / to express their **sincere** thanks, / and to show **humility**. // Let's check each feature / one by one. //

② First, / it is important / for athletes / to **praise** their opponents / at the beginning / of their speeches. // They usually keep eye contact / with their opponents. // For example, / Naomi Osaka, / who won the final match / of the 2018 U.S. Open Championships, / **sincerely** honored her opponent, / Serena Williams. // Serena also did that / in her speech. // It doesn't matter / **whether** they win / or lose. //

③ Second, / many winners acknowledge / their opponents' hard work. // Their opponents **probably** / had to **overcome** / some difficulties / before the tournament, / such as **injuries**, / **slumps** / or frustrations. // For example, / in the 2019 Australian Open Championships, / Naomi said to her opponent, / Petra Kvitová, / "You've been through hardships." // (178 words)

🔊 **音読しよう**

スピーキング・トレーナー

Practice 1　スラッシュ位置で文を区切って読んでみよう ☐
Practice 2　英語の強弱のリズムに注意して読んでみよう ☐
TRY!　　　 1分50秒以内に本文全体を音読しよう ☐

📖 **Reading**　本文の内容を読んで理解しよう【知識・技能】【思考力・判断力・表現力】　　共通テスト

Make the correct choice to complete each sentence or answer each question. (各4点)

1. Which of the following is **not** mentioned in the passage as the features of athletes' victory speeches? ☐

   ① To explain how hard they worked to win the game.

   ② To express their appreciation.

   ③ To show respect for the people they played against in the game.

   ④ To show that they are not perfect.

2. One **opinion** stated in the passage is that ☐ .

   ① Naomi Osaka honored Serena Williams in her speech

   ② Naomi Osaka won the 2018 U.S. Open Championships

   ③ Serena Williams honored Naomi Osaka in her speech

   ④ praising their opponents is important for athletes

英語の強弱のリズムを理解して音読することができる。
スピーチの特徴に関する英文を読んで，概要や要点を捉えることができる。
文脈を理解して適切な語句を用いて英文を完成することができる。
平易な英語で話される短い英文を聞いて必要な情報を聞き取ることができる。 簡単な語句を用いてお祝いの言葉に返答することができる。
スポーツでの成功について簡単な語句を用いて考えを表現することができる。

oals

3. In the 2019 Australian Open Championships, Petra Kvitová ⬜.

① congratulated Naomi Osaka for winning the tournament

② defeated Naomi Osaka after overcoming her hardships

③ proved that overcoming the difficulties is the key to success

④ was praised for overcoming difficulties though she didn't win the tournament

🔍 Vocabulary & Grammar　重要表現や文法事項について理解しよう【知識】　英検® GTEC®

Make the correct choice to complete each sentence.（各2点）

1. The temples in Japan (　　　) visitors from all over the world.

　① attract　　　② chase　　　③ overcome　　　④ support

2. (　　　) I can attend the party or not depends on my physical condition that day.

　① When　　　② Where　　　③ Whether　　　④ Who

3. Take an umbrella with you. It will (　　　) rain today.

　① completely　　② never　　　③ probably　　　④ really

4. Careless use of this machine can cause serious (　　　).

　① business　　　② illness　　　③ injury　　　④ success

5. Martin, (　　　) father is Japanese, speaks English and Japanese fluently.

　① to whom　　　② who　　　③ whom　　　④ whose

🎧 Listening　英文を聞いて理解しよう【知識・技能】【思考力・判断力・表現力】　共通テスト CD 21

Listen to the English and make the best choice to match the content.（4点）

　① Mika has been practicing table tennis with the speaker.

　② The speaker and Mika won the tournament three years ago.

　③ The speaker is practicing hard to win against Mika.

💬 Interaction　英文を聞いて会話を続けよう【知識・技能】【思考力・判断力・表現力】　スピーキング・トレーナー CD 22

Listen to the English and respond to the last remark.（7点）

　［メモ　　　　　　　　　　　　　　　　　　　　　　　　　　　　　　　　　　　　］

　アドバイス　何かを聞かれているわけではないが，自分ならどう返答するか考えよう。

✏️ Production（Write）　自分の考えを書いて伝えよう【思考力・判断力・表現力】

Write your answer to the following question.（7点）

　What do you think is the most important thing for success in sports?

　アドバイス　正解はないので，自分が最も大切だと思うことは何か，考えてみよう。

④　Third, / players often thank / all of their fans / and supporters. // There are always coaches, / teammates, / trainers, / managers / and **nutritionists** / behind a professional athlete. // They are all working together / as a team. // Besides them, / many **staff** members, / such as judges, / officials, / **sponsors** and ball kids, / are essential / to **organize** a tournament. // If these people did not support athletes, / there couldn't be a tournament. //

⑤　In the 2019 Rugby World Cup / in Japan, / South Africa **defeated** England / in the final game. // Siya Kolisi, / who was the captain, / expressed his gratitude / to his own country, / South Africa, / in his victory interview. // He said to people / in his country, / "I cannot thank you enough. // I'm so grateful / to all the people / in South Africa / for cheering for us." //

⑥　The baseball player / Shohei Otani / was named **Rookie** of the Year / in 2018. // In his speech / at the **awards ceremony**, / he thanked all the people / **concerned** with the award / he received. // They were the people / hosting the great event, / the baseball writers voting for him, / the **entire** Angels **organization**, / his fans, / and his parents. // （177 words）

🔊 **音読しよう**
Practice 1　スラッシュ位置で文を区切って読んでみよう ☐
Practice 2　英語の強弱のリズムに注意して読んでみよう ☐
TRY!　　　１分50秒以内に本文全体を音読しよう ☐

スピーキング・トレーナー

📖 **Reading**　本文の内容を読んで理解しよう【知識・技能】【思考力・判断力・表現力】　　共通テスト

Make the correct choice to complete each sentence or answer each question. （各4点）

1.　Players thank staff members such as judges or officials because ☐ .
　　① they are necessary to realize the tournament
　　② they are always working together as a team
　　③ players want to be friendly with them to win the game
　　④ supporting athletes is not fun job

2.　Siya Kolisi says ☐ .
　　① he cannot be too grateful to people in South Africa
　　② he could be the captain of the team thanks to people in South Africa
　　③ he is proud of his team and opponent team which played the great game
　　④ South Africa won the World Cup because he cheered for the team

3. Which of the following is **not** true about Shohei Otani? ☐

　① Many baseball writers were happy to choose Shohei as Rookie of the Year.

　② Shohei expressed his gratitude to all the people concerned with the award.

　③ Shohei hosted an awards ceremony for the Rookie of the Year.

　④ Shohei made a speech when he was named Rookie of the Year.

🔍 Vocabulary & Grammar　重要表現や文法事項について理解しよう【知識】　　英検® GTEC®

Make the correct choice to complete each sentence. (各2点)

1. One of his jobs is to (　　　　) company trips every two years.

　① invite　　　　② organize　　　　③ suggest　　　　④ think

2. In the World Cup, France (　　　　) Belgium and reached the final.

　① cheered for　　② defeated　　　　③ lost　　　　④ won

3. The war between the two countries affected the (　　　) world.

　① all　　　　② entire　　　　③ through　　　　④ total

4. The book is (　　　) mainly with the merits and demerits of urban development.

　① applied　　　② concerned　　　③ interested　　　④ voted

5. If I (　　　) enough money, I could buy the latest smartphone.

　① could have　　② had　　　　③ have　　　　④ have had

🎧 Listening　英文を聞いて理解しよう【知識・技能】【思考力・判断力・表現力】　共通テスト　CD 23

Listen to the English and make the best choice to match the content. (4点)

　① He doesn't get angry with his fans taking his photos.

　② He doesn't mind taking pictures after the game.

　③ His fans must not take his picture.

💬 Interaction　英文を聞いて会話を続けよう【知識・技能】【思考力・判断力・表現力】　スピーキング・トレーナー　CD 24

Listen to the English and respond to the last remark. (7点)

［メモ　　］

　アドバイス　最初の発言はあなたの発言です。相手と同じ情報量で返答するように心がけよう。

✏️ Production（Write）　自分の考えを書いて伝えよう【思考力・判断力・表現力】

Write your answer to the following question. (7点)

　Has anyone thanked you recently?

　アドバイス　何をしたときに感謝されたか，具体的に書こう。

⑦ Finally, / showing humility / is a **technique** / quite unique to the speeches / of professional athletes. // They **intentionally confess** / their worries or **weaknesses** / in their speeches, / which hurts no one / and makes a **favorable impression** / on listeners. // Being **humble** / can be difficult, / but athletes often use / this technique / in their speeches. //

⑧ At the awards ceremony / for Rookie of the Year, / Shohei Otani was holding / his notes for his speech. // He looked down at them **frequently** / during his speech. // However, / he finished his speech / with the sentence, / "**Hopefully**, / I will not need this **cheat** sheet / the next time I'm up here." // Showing humility / made his **audience** laugh / at just the right time. //

⑨ You can learn / what professional athletes think / by looking at these four special features / in their victory speeches. // When you deliver a speech / in English, / you can use some of these techniques / to make your speech / more **impressive**. // If you **analyze** / athletes' **outstanding** speeches, / you too can become a speaker / who is attractive / to your audience. // (165 words)

◀)) 音読しよう   スピーキング・トレーナー
Practice 1   スラッシュ位置で文を区切って読んでみよう ☐
Practice 2   英語の強弱のリズムに注意して読んでみよう ☐
TRY!   1分40秒以内に本文全体を音読しよう ☐

📖 **Reading**   本文の内容を読んで理解しよう【知識・技能】【思考力・判断力・表現力】   共通テスト

Make the correct choice to complete each sentence. (各4点)

1. Showing humility in the speeches ☐.
    ① is quite a popular technique for all speakers
    ② is not difficult because all athletes have worries or weaknesses
    ③ leads to make good impression of the speaker
    ④ means that the athlete hurts no one

2. Shohei Otani ☐.
    ① didn't speak English well, but he kept eye contact with the audience
    ② doesn't need any help in his speech
    ③ is not so good at making speeches in English
    ④ speaks English so well that he can make people laugh in his speeches

3. To make your speech attractive, you ☐.
    ① can learn from athletes' speeches   ② have to win the tournament first
    ③ should have your own way of speaking   ④ should practice like athletes do

◀) 英語の強弱のリズムを理解して音読することができる。
□ スピーチの特徴に関する英文を読んで，概要や要点を捉えることができる。
♀ 文脈を理解して適切な語句を用いて英文を完成することができる。
○ 平易な英語で話される短い英文を聞いて必要な情報を聞き取ることができる。
♀ 人間関係について簡単な語句を用いて説明することができる。
als ♀ 謙虚さについて簡単な語句を用いて考えを表現することができる。

🔍 Vocabulary & Grammar 　重要表現や文法事項について理解しよう【知識】　英検® GTEC®

Make the correct choice to complete each sentence. (各2点)

1. She (　　　) that she had eaten his cake.
   ① boasted　　　② confessed　　　③ got angry　　　④ promised

2. The buses run less (　　　) on weekends.
   ① frequency　　② frequent　　　③ frequentative　　④ frequently

3. The (　　　) at the concert was excited by the performance.
   ① audience　　② clients　　　③ noise　　　④ visitors

4. The idea may be (　　　) to you, but not to everyone.
   ① attract　　　② attracted　　　③ attraction　　　④ attractive

5. I climbed (　　　) is the highest mountain in Japan.
   ① Mt. Fuji, that　② Mt. Fuji, where　③ Mt. Fuji, which　④ Mt. Fuji which

🎧 Listening 　英文を聞いて理解しよう【知識・技能】【思考力・判断力・表現力】　共通テスト　CD 25

Listen to the English and make the best choice to match the content. (4点)

① The speaker is feeling nervous before her speech.

② The speaker is making a speech in a hall.

③ The speaker is planning to give a lecture to students.

💬 Interaction 　英文を聞いて会話を続けよう【知識・技能】【思考力・判断力・表現力】　スピーキング・トレーナー　CD 26

Listen to the English and respond to the last remark. (7点)

［メモ 　　　　　　　　　　　　　　　　　　　　　　　　　　　　　　　　　　]

アドバイス　とくに思い当たることがない場合でも，どうしたいかなどを答えよう。

✐ Production (Write) 　自分の考えを書いて伝えよう【思考力・判断力・表現力】

Write your answer to the following question. (7点)

Do you think being humble is important? Why or why not?

アドバイス　そうではない行動をしたときのことを想像してみると考えやすい。arrogant「横柄な，傲慢な」

29

You found a victory speech / by the tennis player / Roger Federer / on the Internet. // You are listening to it. //

Roger's speech / after his final match / against Marin Cilic / (**Croatia**) / in the 2017 Wimbledon Championships //

Marin Cilic / is a hero. // **Congratulations** / on his running second. // He played perfectly / in the final, / but it was a bad result / for him. // I really hope / there will be another good result / for him / in the future. //

I can't believe / I was able to win / without losing any sets. // There were times / when I couldn't believe / I could take part in the final. // However, / I decided / to believe it. // And Marin and I did it! // It was a great time / to be able to **compete** / with Marin here / today. // The center court / was filled with a lot of **spectators** / and had a great **atmosphere**. // I will be back here / again / next year. //

My little sons, / watching from their seats, / don't know what's going on. // They might think / this place is a good playground. // My daughters understand this situation / a little, / but I will have to talk to them / about this / again. // I'm so grateful / to my family / for supporting me! // I couldn't have played / in such a wonderful match / if I hadn't had / your great support. // Thank you again / very much. // (216 words)

🔊 **音読しよう**　　　　　　　　　　　　　　　　　　　スピーキング・トレーナー

Practice 1　スラッシュ位置で文を区切って読んでみよう □
Practice 2　英語の強弱のリズムに注意して読んでみよう □
TRY!　　　　2分10秒以内に本文全体を音読しよう □

📖 **Reading**　本文の内容を読んで理解しよう【知識・技能】【思考力・判断力・表現力】　　共通テスト

Make the correct choice to complete each sentence or answer each question. (各6点)

1. Roger Federer ☐.

   ① almost lost to Cilic in the final but eventually won

   ② and Marin Cilic advanced to the finals as a doubles pair

   ③ couldn't take part in the final

   ④ was happy to play with Cilic in the final

2. Which of the following is true? ☐

   ① Federer could not perform well because of the little support of his family.

   ② Federer's daughters are proud of their father's success and will never forget it.

   ③ The final stage was a good playground for Federer's little sons.

   ④ The speech included encouragement for his opponents and appreciation to his family.

🔍 Vocabulary & Grammar   重要表現や文法事項について理解しよう【知識】   英検® GTEC®

Make the correct choice to complete each sentence. (各2点)

1. (   ) on your entrance to the university!

① Congratulate   ② Congratulation   ③ Congratulations   ④ Congratulatory

2. It's difficult for our small clothing shop to (   ) Uniqlo.

① advertise   ② beat with   ③ compete with   ④ cooperate with

3. More than 20,000 (   ) came to the stadium to watch that soccer game.

① audience   ② participants   ③ players   ④ spectators

4. Our staff are all friendly and you can work in a relaxed (   ) in our office.

① air   ② atmosphere   ③ scene   ④ state

5. It is important to see what is going (   ) in the world.

① at   ② by   ③ for   ④ on

6. He said he had nothing to do with the incident, (   ) is unbelievable.

① it   ② this   ③ what   ④ which

7. If more people used public transportation instead of private cars, (   ) less pollution.

① it will be   ② it would be   ③ there will be   ④ there would be

8. If I (   ) the courage to consider other options then, I would not have faced these difficulties.

① had   ② had had   ③ had have   ④ have had

🎧 Listening   英文を聞いて理解しよう【知識・技能】【思考力・判断力・表現力】   共通テスト   CD 27

Listen to the English and make the best choice to match the content. (各4点)

1. When did the speaker win the tournament before?

① One and a half years ago   ② Two and a half years ago

③ Two years ago   ④ Three years ago

2. What kept the speaker away from skating?

① Her broken leg did.   ② Her injured left arm did.

③ Her mental health did.   ④ Her father's illness did.

3. Which of the following is true about her family?

① Her father educated her coach.

② Her father treated her leg in the hospital.

③ Her mother coached her.

④ Her mother helped her with rehabilitation work.

You join an international event / about **disaster prevention**. // You find a poster. //

There Are More Disasters / These Days! //

We often hear sad news / about heavy rains, / **typhoons** / and earthquakes. // They are **constantly** happening / all over the world. // People are suffering. // Their houses are destroyed. // They have **nowhere** to go. // "They" may be "you" / tomorrow. //

The graph shows / how many natural disasters have been reported / around the world / since 1990. // It may be true / that past disasters are **underreported**. // However, / it seems / that the number has increased / **recently**. // Some **researchers suggest** / that climate change has something to do / with this increase. //

Typical examples of natural disasters include floods, / **droughts**, / storms, / **volcanic eruptions** / and earthquakes. // They have caused the deaths of millions of people / as well as huge economic **losses**. // What can we do / to deal with these disasters? // Now is the time / to act seriously / on this global issue. // (148 words)

🔊 音読しよう　　　　　　　　　　　　　　　　　　スピーキング・トレーナー

Practice 1　スラッシュ位置で文を区切って読んでみよう☐
Practice 2　イントネーションに注意して読んでみよう☐
TRY!　　　　1分30秒以内に本文全体を音読しよう☐

📖 **Reading**　本文の内容を読んで理解しよう【知識・技能】【思考力・判断力・表現力】　　共通テスト

Make the correct choice to complete each sentence or answer each question. (各4点)

1. Which of the following is probably true? ☐

① The number of natural disasters was the largest in 1980.

② The number of natural disasters decreased gradually.

③ The number of natural disasters in 1995 was smaller than that in 2015.

④ The number of natural disasters in 2015 was smaller than that in 1995.

2. According to this poster, natural disasters have caused ☐.

① a lot of deaths, injuries and terrible economic situations

② a lot of traffic accidents everywhere

③ huge economic losses only

④ terrible climate change

3. What is the message that the writer wants to tell us most? ☐

① Let's act seriously on natural disaster problems together.

② Let's make a graph of the number of natural disasters.

③ Let's research the number of natural disasters.

④ Let's study about climate change.

🔍 Vocabulary & Grammar　重要表現や文法事項について理解しよう【知識】　英検® GTEC®

Make the correct choice to complete each sentence. (各2点)

1. My older brother researches earthquakes at university and hopes to work at the
   (　　　) Control Center in America.
   ① Disappointed　　② Disaster　　③ Distance　　④ Divided

2. We discussed (　　　) and treatment of diseases at the conference.
   ① prevention　　② production　　③ prohibition　　④ promotion

3. The shortage of rain brought a serious (　　　) to East Africa and killed many
   animals last year.
   ① drought　　② earthquake　　③ flood　　④ typhoon

4. The young CEO suffered a large (　　　) in his business so he had to leave the
   company.
   ① loss　　② lost　　③ profit　　④ winning

5. Amy got up late this morning so she must (　　　) the train.
   ① have been missed　　② have caught　　③ have missed　　④ missed

🎧 Listening　英文を聞いて理解しよう【知識・技能】【思考力・判断力・表現力】　共通テスト CD 28

Listen to the English and make the best choice to match the content. (4点)

① The area hasn't had large earthquakes for more than 50 years.

② The researcher experienced a large earthquake there about 80 years ago.

③ The speaker found that no large earthquakes happened there these days.

💬 Interaction　英文を聞いて会話を続けよう【知識・技能】【思考力・判断力・表現力】　スピーキング・トレーナー CD 29

Listen to the English and respond to the last remark. (7点)

　［メモ　　　　　　　　　　　　　　　　　　　　　　　　　　　　　　　　　　　　　］

　　アドバイス　知っている場合は，それが何かを答えよう。

💬 Production (Speak)　自分の考えを話して伝えよう【思考力・判断力・表現力】　スピーキング・トレーナー

Speak out your answer to the following question. (7点)

　Do you do anything to prepare for disasters?

　　アドバイス　どんな場合に備えて何をしているかを答えよう。

More and more natural disasters / seem to be happening / around the world. // Are you well prepared / to reduce your own risk / from future disasters? //

① Different **regions** in the world / have unique types of natural disasters. // Africa tends to suffer / from droughts. // In **Latin America**, / earthquakes and tsunamis **occur** / frequently. // Asia is likely / to suffer **damage** / from floods / and storms. //

② Japan is known / to have suffered from natural disasters / frequently / and **severely**. // Earthquakes and typhoons / in **particular** / have affected our lives. // Earthquakes in Japan / account for about 20 percent / of the world's **occurrences** / with a **magnitude** of six / or higher. // Typhoons bring strong winds / and heavy rains, / resulting in flooding / and **landslides**. // Climate change may be increasing / the risk of disasters. //

③ Traditional approaches / to disaster prevention / and risk **management** / may not be enough. // We have developed **infrastructure** / such as roads, / buildings / and **dams**. // We have also trained ourselves / through **evacuation** drills / at school / and in communities. // Even so, / natural disasters still continue / to destroy life / and **property**. // What else can we do / to deal with future disasters? //

(176 words)

🔊 **音読しよう**   スピーキング・トレーナー

Practice 1   スラッシュ位置で文を区切って読んでみよう☐
Practice 2   イントネーションに注意して読んでみよう☐
TRY!   1分50秒以内に本文全体を音読しよう☐

📖 **Reading**   本文の内容を読んで理解しよう【知識・技能】【思考力・判断力・表現力】   共通テスト

Make the correct choice to complete each sentence or answer each question. (各4点)

1. Typhoons with strong winds and heavy rains often lead to ☐.
   ① droughts and earthquakes   ② earthquakes and tsunamis
   ③ flooding and landslides   ④ volcanic eruption and wildfire

2. According to paragraph 3, ☐ may not be enough.
   ① new approaches to disaster prevention
   ② traditional approaches to disaster prevention and financial management
   ③ traditional ways of disaster prevention and risk management
   ④ traditional ways to protect our property

3. As one of the traditional approaches to disaster prevention, what have we done at school? ☐
   ① We have checked the water level of dams.
   ② We have developed infrastructure.
   ③ We have done evacuation drills.
   ④ We have kept enough foods.

🔊 イントネーションを理解して音読することができる。
📖 自然災害の特徴と防災に関する英文を読んで，概要や要点を捉えることができる。
🔍 文脈を理解して適切な語句を用いて英文を完成することができる。
🎧 平易な英語で話される短い英文を聞いて必要な情報を聞き取ることができる。
💬 避難訓練について簡単な語句を用いて考えを表現することができる。　　✍ 避難バッグについて簡単な語句を用いて説明することができる。

oals

🔍 Vocabulary & Grammar　重要表現や文法事項について理解しよう【知識】　英検® GTEC®

Make the correct choice to complete each sentence.（各2点）

1.　The city was (　　　) damaged by the big typhoon.
　　① separately　　　② severely　　　③ similarly　　　④ strictly

2.　Mr. Tanaka owns a large amount of (　　　) and runs several companies in Osaka.
　　① parliaments　　② patients　　③ promotions　　④ property

3.　The graph shows that smokers (　　　) for more than 80% of male adults in 1980.
　　① abandoned　　② accounted　　③ announced　　④ appointed

4.　A: Do you have any plans for tonight?
　　B: No.　I have nothing (　　　) particular.
　　① in　　　　　② of　　　　　③ on　　　　　④ with

5.　Patrick seems to (　　　) a bad cold because he got wet in the rain last night.
　　① catch　　　② had caught　　③ have been caught　　④ have caught

🎧 Listening　英文を聞いて理解しよう【知識・技能】【思考力・判断力・表現力】　共通テスト　CD 30

Listen to the English and make the best choice to match the content.（4点）

　　① Bridges to the town didn't work after the typhoon.
　　② Much rainwater came into the small town.
　　③ The storm broke the two small towns.

💬 Interaction　英文を聞いて会話を続けよう【知識・技能】【思考力・判断力・表現力】　スピーキング・トレーナー　CD 31

Listen to the English and respond to the last remark.（7点）

　　［メ モ　　］

　　アドバイス　まずは相手の質問に明確に答えて，その理由などを付け加えよう。

✏ Production（Write）　自分の考えを書いて伝えよう【思考力・判断力・表現力】

Write your answer to the following question.（7点）

　　Do you have an emergency bag?　What is in it?

　　アドバイス　持っていない場合は，何を入れておけばよいか想像して答える。

----

4 Recent ideas and technologies / allow us to prepare / for disasters. // For example, / you may have heard / about **hazard** maps. // They tell you / the nearest evacuation sites / in the areas / where disasters are likely to occur. // Learning about the area / where you live **beforehand**, / or even after a disaster has happened, / will help you **avoid** / potential risks / in the future. //

5 **Emergency** food is also gaining **popularity**. // Nowadays, / you can buy / a variety of foods, / such as easy-to-make rice, / **pre-packaged** curry / and canned bread. // They can be eaten / with little **preparation** / and stored / for a couple of years. // It is said / that you should store / a **minimum** of a three-day supply of food. // Of course, / you can eat the food / as part of your daily meals / before the food's best-before date. //

6 In addition, / you need to think / about what to do / if the power goes out. // An emergency radio / can keep you **updated** / with disaster information. // Some radios are **rechargeable** / with solar panels / or hand **cranks**. // You can use such a radio / not only as an emergency **flashlight** / but also as a battery **charger** / for your **digital** devices. // Having such a power source / will make a big difference. //

(196 words)

🔊 音読しよう

Practice 1　スラッシュ位置で文を区切って読んでみよう □
Practice 2　イントネーションに注意して読んでみよう □
TRY!　　　 2分以内に本文全体を音読しよう □

スピーキング・トレーナー

📖 **Reading**　本文の内容を読んで理解しよう【知識・技能】【思考力・判断力・表現力】　共通テスト

Make the correct choice to complete each sentence or answer each question. (各4点)

1. By ⬚, we may be able to avoid potential risks in the future.

① exchanging recent ideas with people in other countries

② making hazard maps on our own

③ preparing recent technology with our neighbors

④ using hazard maps to learn about our area

2. Which of the following is true about emergency food? ⬚

① It can be stored for a few years.

② It shouldn't be eaten as our daily meals.

③ It takes a lot of time to prepare a pre-packed curry.

④ There are not many kinds of emergency food.

3. If the power goes out, ⬚.

① an emergency radio can be exchangeable for cash

② an emergency radio can be used as a phone

③ an emergency radio can help you get the latest information

④ an emergency radio can provide you popular music

◀) イントネーションを理解して音読することができる。　　　　📖 防災に関する英文を読んで，概要や要点を捉えることができる。
🔍 文脈を理解して適切な語句を用いて英文を完成することができる。
🎧 平易な英語で話される短い英文を聞いて必要な情報を聞き取ることができる。
🗣 停電について簡単な語句を用いて説明することができる。
✎ ハザードマップについて簡単な語句を用いて考えを表現することができる。

🔍 Vocabulary & Grammar　重要表現や文法事項について理解しよう【知識】　　英検® GTEC®

Make the correct choice to complete each sentence. (各2点)

1. A: Could you send me an e-mail (　　　　)?

   B: OK, I will.

   ① after　　　　　　② beforehand　　　　　③ prior　　　　　④ with hands

2. Tom tried to (　　　　) making the same mistakes.

   ① avoid　　　　　　② enjoy　　　　　　　③ finish　　　　　④ give up

3. Last night, all the lights in our house went (　　　　) and my daughter started crying.

   ① on　　　　　　　② out　　　　　　　　③ to　　　　　　　④ up

4. This latest cloth (　　　　) air to pass through very easily.

   ① allows　　　　　　② applies　　　　　　③ arrives　　　　　④ assumes

5. Emma is angry at you. You should (　　　　) her the truth at that time.

   ① have been told　② have told　　　　　③ not tell　　　　④ tell

🎧 Listening　英文を聞いて理解しよう【知識・技能】【思考力・判断力・表現力】　共通テスト　CD 32

Listen to the English and make the best choice to match the content. (4点)

   ① Flood may happen in some areas of the map.

   ② The map says the speaker's house is in dangerous area.

   ③ The speaker's parents are well prepared for the flood.

🗣 Interaction　英文を聞いて会話を続けよう【知識・技能】【思考力・判断力・表現力】　スピーキング・トレーナー　CD 33

Listen to the English and respond to the last remark. (7点)

   アドバイス　何が困るか，想像してみよう。

   [メモ　　　　　　　　　　　　　　　　　　　　　　　　　　　　　　　　　]

✎ Production (Write)　自分の考えを書いて伝えよう【思考力・判断力・表現力】

Write your answer to the following question. (7点)

   Have you ever checked the hazard map of the area where you live?

   アドバイス　確認してどうだったか，なぜ確認していないかなどの情報を加えよう。

----

⑦ We should also be **aware** of / who is at risk / in disasters. // You may think of elderly people, / little children / or **physically-challenged** people, / but you should also think of visitors / from foreign countries. // Such visitors may have never experienced / an earthquake / before. // Some of them cannot understand Japanese. // In fact, / visitors are said to have **struggled** / to find **proper** information / in their own languages / in past earthquakes / in Japan. //

⑧ In order to help foreign people / at risk, / the use of **pictograms** and **plain** Japanese words / has gained attention / recently. // These communication tools use / **illustrations** and simple expressions / so that everybody can understand / their messages / easily. // Some disaster information is also available / in foreign languages, / such as English, / Chinese / and Korean, / **via** websites, / **apps** / and social **media**. // Such information can help everyone / in a disaster. //

⑨ Recent ideas and technologies / have improved our chances / to survive disasters. // However, / it is up to each of us / to make full use of them. // What if / a big earthquake happens / now? // What can you do / for yourself, / your family / and people around you? // It is never too early / to get prepared. // (186 words)

🔊 音読しよう

Practice 1　スラッシュ位置で文を区切って読んでみよう □
Practice 2　イントネーションに注意して読んでみよう □
TRY!　　　1分50秒以内に本文全体を音読しよう □

スピーキング・トレーナー

📖 **Reading**　本文の内容を読んで理解しよう【知識・技能】【思考力・判断力・表現力】　　共通テスト

Make the correct choice to complete each sentence or answer each question. (各4点)

1. Visitors from foreign countries ⬚ in past earthquakes in Japan.

① have had trouble getting the appropriate and correct information

② have had trouble staying at evacuation sites with local residents

③ have struggled to find their hotels where they were staying at

④ have struggled to get meals of their own countries

2. Why has the use of illustrations and simple expressions gained attention? ⬚

① Because drawing and writing them takes less time.

② Because everyone can understand the messages easily.

③ Because there are few people who speak English in Japan.

④ Because tourists are usually from developing countries

3. Which of the following is true as the message from Lesson 4? ⬚

① It is never too early to get prepared for disasters.

② It is too late to get prepared for disasters.

③ We don't need to prepare for disasters.

④ We have already prepared enough for disasters.

🔍 Vocabulary & Grammar　重要表現や文法事項について理解しよう【知識】　英検® GTEC®

Make the correct choice to complete each sentence. (各2点)

1. You should think of (　　　　) clothes to wear in the office.
   ① political　　　② precious　　　③ principal　　　④ proper

2. I gave up passing the exam. I was (　　　　) of my weakness.
   ① alike　　　② alive　　　③ awake　　　④ aware

3. Eating too much at night will put you (　　　) of obesity.
   ① at least　　　② at risk　　　③ in danger　　　④ in need

4. My boss advised that I should (　　　) my unique experience for the new job.
   ① make　　　② make sure of　　　③ make use　　　④ make use of

5. The hurricane is said to (　　　) the small island.
   ① be destroyed　　② destroy　　　③ have been destroyed　　④ have destroyed

🎧 Listening　英文を聞いて理解しよう【知識・技能】【思考力・判断力・表現力】　共通テスト　CD 34

Listen to the English and make the best choice to match the content. (4点)

① After the earthquake, the city office employed a Spanish staff.

② An earthquake has hit a city in Spain.

③ The city office had no staff who could speak Spanish.

💬 Interaction　英文を聞いて会話を続けよう【知識・技能】【思考力・判断力・表現力】　スピーキング・トレーナー　CD 35

Listen to the English and respond to the last remark. (7点)

[メモ　　　　　　　　　　　　　　　　　　　　　　　　　　　　　　　　　　　　　　]

アドバイス　相手がたずねたいことは，見たことがあるか，ないかだけではないことに注意しよう。

✒️ Production (Write)　自分の考えを書いて伝えよう【思考力・判断力・表現力】

Write your answer to the following question. (7点)

Have you downloaded any disaster prevention apps? What functions do they have?

アドバイス　各地の地震速報を知らせるアプリや，天気予報アプリなども含めてもよいでしょう。

A teacher gave students the following **task**. // Koji is now making a **brief** presentation / about his idea. // After that, / Airi asks some questions. //

TASK /

What items can you create / with limited **resources** / in case of a disaster? // Your ideas and knowledge / will be important / in such a situation. // By using the materials below, / develop some original items / that might be useful / if you are faced / with a natural disaster. //

Koji: My idea / is to make a "**cardboard** bed." // In case of a disaster, / you may need / to **evacuate** from your home / and spend several nights / in a school **gymnasium**, / for example. // You can create a bed / with twelve cardboard boxes, / twelve pieces of cardboard, / and some packaging tape. // The bed can help you stay warm / during the night. // What do you think / about my idea? //

Airi: That's a great idea, / Koji. // Can the bed **withstand** the weight of an adult? //

Koji: Thank you / for your question. // Yes, / it can. // I forgot to tell you, / but you can put the pieces of cardboard **diagonally** / into each box / to **reinforce** the bed. //

Airi: I see. // You then **seal** each box / with some packaging tape, / right? //

Koji: Yes. // Just putting 12 boxes together / creates a bed. // You can also cover it / with cloth, / if you have some. // (209 words)

🔊 **音読しよう**　　　　　　　　　　　　　　　　　スピーキング・トレーナー

Practice 1　スラッシュ位置で文を区切って読んでみよう ☐
Practice 2　イントネーションに注意して読んでみよう ☐
TRY!　　　2分10秒以内に本文全体を音読しよう ☐

📖 **Reading**　本文の内容を読んで理解しよう【知識・技能】【思考力・判断力・表現力】　　共通テスト

Make the correct choice to complete each sentence or answer each question. (各4点)

1. According to Koji, what do we need to make a cardboard bed? ☐
   ① Twelve cardboard and some packaging tape.
   ② Twelve cardboard boxes, some packaging tape and a cloth.
   ③ Twelve cardboard boxes, twelve cardboard and a cloth.
   ④ Twelve cardboard boxes, twelve pieces of cardboard, and some packaging tape.

2. We need to ☐ to make the bed stronger.
   ① put the pieces of cardboard diagonally into each box
   ② put the pieces of cardboard vertically into each box
   ③ seal each box with some packaging tape diagonally
   ④ seal each box with some packaging tape vertically

3. If you have some ☐, you can cover the bed with it.
   ① cloth　　　　　② newspaper　　　　③ plastic bag　　　④ towel

Vocabulary & Grammar 重要表現や文法事項について理解しよう【知識】 英検 GTEC

Make the correct choice to complete each sentence. (各2点)

1. The host of XYZ TV had a (　　　) interview with the singer before the actual one.
   ① formal　　　② visual　　　③ bloody　　　④ brief

2. The moving company always uses recyclable (　　　) boxes because it is eco-friendly.
   ① boarding　　② cardboard　　③ cardboards　　④ white board

3. The researcher says that the material can (　　　) big changes in temperature.
   ① withdraw　　② withhold　　③ withstand　　④ within

4. (　　　) fire, we must use this exit and stairs.
   ① In addition to　② In case of　③ In contrast to　④ In spite of

5. Nancy has a lot of tasks to do today. She is (　　　) a stressful situation.
   ① faced by　　② faced in　　③ faced on　　④ faced with

6. A: I am shocked that Eric told a lie to me.
   B: You (　　　) have trusted him because he is an infamous liar.
   ① could　　② couldn't　　③ should　　④ shouldn't

7. Cathy is believed to (　　　) a great singer when she was in her twenties.
   ① be　　② been　　③ have been　　④ had been

8. Roads are wet. It must (　　　) last night.
   ① be raining　② have rained　③ rain　④ rained

Listening 英文を聞いて理解しよう【知識・技能】【思考力・判断力・表現力】 共通テスト CD 36

Listen to the English and make the best choice to match the content. (各4点)

1. What happened to Pompeii in A.D. 62?
   ① An earthquake　　② Floods
   ③ Two kinds of disasters　④ Volcanic eruptions

2. When did the volcanic eruption occur?
   ① Around A.D. 45
   ② Five years after the earthquake
   ③ In A.D. 62
   ④ Seventeen years after the earthquake

3. Which of the following is true about the volcanic disaster in Pompeii?
   ① Melted rocks came after fallen stones and rocks.
   ② Pompeii was rebuilt by the survivors of the disaster.
   ③ The heat from the river killed people in Pompeii.
   ④ The mountain in the southwest of Pompeii caused it.

As a group project, / you are studying / the system of the **imperial era** name / in Japan. // On the Internet, / you found a news clip / about "Reiwa" / and some posts / about how people abroad saw / the **dawn** of the new era. //

Good afternoon. // The name of the new era / in Japan / has just been **announced**. // The name of the new era / that follows Heisei / will be "Reiwa"! // The **Chief Cabinet Secretary** / is now holding up a white card / with the new name written / in two characters / in black ink. // "Reiwa" comes from characters / used in an **introduction** / to some poems / in the *Manyoshu*, / an ancient **anthology** / of Japanese **poetry**. // This **introductory passage mentions** / soft winds and *ume* **blossoms** / in spring. //

Victor: What does the new name "Reiwa" / mean? //

Hiroshi: "Reiwa" is made up of two characters, / "rei" and "wa." / "Rei" can mean "beautiful" / or "good." // "Wa" can mean "harmony." // The Japanese government made an official announcement / about the English meaning of "Reiwa." // It is "the era of beautiful harmony." //

Wei: Will Japan choose a beautiful harmony of peace / in the new era / of "Reiwa"? //

Agatha: People around the world / are now waiting to see / whether Japan will contribute / to world peace / in this new era. // (200 words)

音読しよう

Practice 1　スラッシュ位置で文を区切って読んでみよう□
Practice 2　イントネーションに注意して読んでみよう□
TRY!　　　2分以内に本文全体を音読しよう□

スピーキング・トレーナー

Reading　本文の内容を読んで理解しよう【知識・技能】【思考力・判断力・表現力】　共通テスト

Make the correct choice to complete each sentence. (各4点)

1. The new era name was referred to 　　.
   ① an ancient Chinese story
   ② an official announcement made by the Japanese government
   ③ the ideas from people around the world
   ④ the introduction to some poems in the *Manyoshu*

2. "Reiwa" means 　　.
   ① the order and the sum　　② soft winds and *ume* blossoms in spring
   ③ the era of beautiful harmony　　④ the new world of peace

3. One **opinion** stated in the discussion is that 　　.
   ① people are expecting Japan to contribute to world peace
   ② "Reiwa" is made up of two characters
   ③ the meaning of "Reiwa" was officially explained
   ④ Victor didn't know the meaning of "Reiwa"

🔊 イントネーションを理解して音読することができる。　　　📖 年号に関する英文を読んで，概要や要点を捉えることができる。
🔍 文脈を理解して適切な語句を用いて英文を完成することができる。
🎧 平易な英語で話される短い英文を聞いて必要な情報を聞き取ることができる。　　💬 時代について簡単な語句を用いて考えを表現することができる。
💬 年号の漢字について簡単な語句を用いて考えを表現することができる。

oals

🔍 Vocabulary & Grammar　重要表現や文法事項について理解しよう【知識】　　英検。 GTEC。

Make the correct choice to complete each sentence. (各2点)

1. Mr. and Mrs. Taylor (　　　) the engagement of their daughter.
   ① announced　　　② appealed　　　③ meant　　　④ spoke

2. The novelist's every spoken word was like (　　　).
   ① harmony　　　② musical　　　③ poetry　　　④ scenery

3. Our professor read a (　　　) from his most recent book.
   ① announcement　　② anthology　　　③ language　　　④ passage

4. The daisy opens its (　　　) in the morning and closes them at night.
   ① blossoms　　　② eyes　　　③ roots　　　④ wings

5. He didn't mention (　　　) he bought at the store.
   ① that　　　② what　　　③ which　　　④ why

🎧 Listening　英文を聞いて理解しよう【知識・技能】【思考力・判断力・表現力】　　共通テスト CD 37

Listen to the English and make the best choice to match the content. (4点)

① The speaker experienced the change of the imperial era two years ago.

② The speaker was born in the twenty-fourth year of the Heisei era.

③ The speaker was twenty-two when the Reiwa era began.

💬 Interaction　英文を聞いて会話を続けよう【知識・技能】【思考力・判断力・表現力】　スピーキング・トレーナー　CD 38

Listen to the English and respond to the last remark. (7点)

［メ モ　　　　　　　　　　　　　　　　　　　　　　　　　　　　　　　　]

アドバイス　何時代かを答えるだけではなく，なぜそう思うのかを答えたり，聞き返したりしよう。

💬 Production (Speak)　自分の考えを話して伝えよう【思考力・判断力・表現力】　スピーキング・トレーナー

Speak out your answer to the following question. (7点)

What Chinese characters would you choose for an era name if you were a member of the committee?

アドバイス　なぜその漢字を選ぶのかの理由を考えよう。読み方や形などの観点から考えてもよい。

How has the era name in Japan / been **determined**? // What meaning does it have / to Japanese people? //

① 　The first imperial era in Japan / dates back to Taika / in 645. // The **notion** of imperial era naming / was **established** / in 701, / when the Taiho era began. // The names were **quoted** / from **classical** Chinese **literature**. // Reiwa, / on the other hand, / was taken / from the *Manyoshu*, / the oldest collection of Japanese poetry. //
② 　It is said / that the *Manyoshu* was **compiled** / mainly during the Nara Period, / and it contains / about 4,500 poems. // The **authors ranged** / from celebrated **poets** to **nameless** farmers. // Public servants / living alone far away from their families / also contributed. // When they made poems, / they were able to forget / their everyday work / for a while / and think of their loved ones / at home. //
③ 　The name Reiwa / comes from a line / in an introductory passage / in the *Manyoshu* / which says, / "It is now **auspicious** early spring; / the weather is fine, / and the wind is soft." // This line describes a party / for viewing *ume* blossoms / under a sunny spring sky. // *Ume* blossoms came from China, / and they were new / to the Japanese / at that time. // They enjoyed *ume* blossoms / and made poems / about them. //　(199 words)

🔊 **音読しよう**

Practice 1	スラッシュ位置で文を区切って読んでみよう ☐	
Practice 2	イントネーションに注意して読んでみよう ☐	
TRY!	2分以内に本文全体を音読しよう ☐	

スピーキング・トレーナー

📖 **Reading**　　本文の内容を読んで理解しよう【知識・技能】【思考力・判断力・表現力】　　共通テスト

Make the correct choice to complete each sentence or answer each question. (各4点)

1.　The imperial era names were quoted ☐ in ancient times.
　　① from Japanese poetry anthologies
　　② from classical Chinese literature
　　③ from the *Manyoshu*
　　④ from voices of public servants living alone far away from their families

2.　Which of the following are **not** mentioned as the authors of the *Manyoshu*? ☐
　　① Celebrated poets.　　　　　　　② Emperors in the Nara period.
　　③ Nameless farmers.　　　　　　④ Public servants.

3.　Which of the following is true about the line of the *Manyoshu* which the name "Reiwa" was quoted from? ☐
　　① A public servant living alone far away from his family read the poem.
　　② It describes the loneliness while viewing *ume* blossoms under a sunny spring sky.
　　③ It expresses the joy of viewing *ume* blossoms together under a sunny sky.
　　④ It is about *ume* blossoms, which were familiar to Japanese people at that time.

◀)) イントネーションを理解して音読することができる。　　　　　　　📖 元号の歴史に関する英文を読んで，概要や要点を捉えることができる。
🔍 文脈を理解して適切な語句を用いて英文を完成することができる。
🎧 平易な英語で話される短い英文を聞いて必要な情報を聞き取ることができる。
🗣 好きなフレーズについて簡単な語句を用いて考えを表現することができる。
✍ 和歌や俳句について簡単な語句を用いて説明することができる。

oals

🔍 Vocabulary & Grammar　　重要表現や文法事項について理解しよう【知識】　　　　英検® GTEC®

Make the correct choice to complete each sentence. (各2点)

1. What (　　　　) the gender of a baby?
   ① chooses　　　　② creates　　　　③ determines　　　　④ makes

2. His first song (　　　　) his reputation as a singer.
   ① established　　　② impressed　　　③ recognized　　　④ rejected

3. Shakespeare is my favorite (　　　　).
   ① author　　　　　② composer　　　　③ editor　　　　　④ engineer

4. The children's age (　　　　) from 5 to 15.
   ① came　　　　　② changed　　　　③ differed　　　　④ ranged

5. She was born in Beijing, (　　　　) she still has lots of friends.
   ① that　　　　　② what　　　　　③ why　　　　　④ where

🎧 Listening　　英文を聞いて理解しよう【知識・技能】【思考力・判断力・表現力】　　共通テスト　CD 39

Listen to the English and make the best choice to match the content. (4点)

① Some *Manyoshu* poems were written on the wall by the speaker.

② The speaker could see some *Manyoshu* poems inside the building.

③ There were some books on the *Manyoshu* in the library.

💬 Interaction　　英文を聞いて会話を続けよう【知識・技能】【思考力・判断力・表現力】　スピーキング・トレーナー　CD 40

Listen to the English and respond to the last remark. (7点)

[メモ　　　　　　　　　　　　　　　　　　　　　　　　　　　　　　　]

アドバイス　lyric は「歌詞」という意味。具体的に思いつかなかったら，曲名でもよいので答えよう。

✍ Production（Write）　　自分の考えを書いて伝えよう【思考力・判断力・表現力】

Write your answer to the following question. (7点)

Have you ever composed a *waka* or *haiku*? What was it about?

アドバイス　Yes か No かを明確に答えてから，2つ目の質問に答えよう。compose「(詩など) を書く」。

/40

④　When we look around the world, / we see different notions of eras. // In Western countries, / the birth of Jesus Christ / became the **norm** / in the Gregorian calendar. // In this calendar, / "B.C." means "Before Christ" / and "A.D." means "**Anno Domini**," / which stands for / "in the year of the **Lord**" / in Latin. //

⑤　In ancient China, / **Emperor** Wu started / to name eras / in 114 B.C. // He changed the era names / when **rare** natural **phenomena** appeared / or good things happened. // For example, / it is said / that he changed the era name / after he saw a **comet** in the sky / and after he hunted a white **kylin**, / a **legendary** animal / in ancient China. //

⑥　China was such a large and **influential** country / that neighboring countries followed the Chinese custom / of naming eras. // In Japan, / for example, / Emperor Ichijo / changed the era to Eiso / in 989, / due to the close approach of Halley's Comet. // In 1912, / China **abandoned** the system of era names / and has never used it since. // Japan is now the only country / where both the Gregorian calendar and era names are used. //　(178 words)

🔊 **音読しよう**　　　　　　　　　　　　　　　　　　スピーキング・トレーナー

Practice 1　スラッシュ位置で文を区切って読んでみよう☐
Practice 2　イントネーションに注意して読んでみよう☐
TRY!　　　　1分50秒以内に本文全体を音読しよう☐

📖 **Reading**　本文の内容を読んで理解しよう【知識・技能】【思考力・判断力・表現力】　　共通テスト

Make the correct choice to complete each sentence or answer each question. (各4点)

1. Which of the following is **not** true about notions of the world's eras? ☐

① Emperor Wu started to name eras in 114 B.C.

② In ancient China, era names had to be changed when good things happened.

③ Japan followed the Chinese custom of naming eras.

④ The birth of Jesus Christ became the norm in the Gregorian calendar.

2. Which of the following affected the change of era names in ancient China? (Choose two options. The order does not matter.) ☐・☐

① A comet appeared in the sky.

② Halley's Comet's approached to the earth.

③ The emperor hunted a white kylin.

④ Neighboring countries followed Chinese customs.

3. In 1912, China abandoned the system of era names and ☐.

① has been using entirely new calendar system

② has been using Japanese era names

③ has never used it since

④ is now considering restoring the custom again

🔍 Vocabulary & Grammar　重要表現や文法事項について理解しよう【知識】　　英検® GTEC®

Make the correct choice to complete each sentence. (各2点)

1. Getting driver's license at 16 is the (　　　　) in the U.S.
   ① crime　　　　② duty　　　　③ norm　　　　④ rule

2. It is (　　　) that he should make such a mistake.
   ① common　　　② nice　　　③ polite　　　④ rare

3. The movement was (　　　) in bringing women's issue into public consciousness.
   ① incredible　　② influential　　③ international　　④ irresponsible

4. UN (　　　) for the United Nations.
   ① makes　　　② means　　　③ stands　　　④ takes

5. It is possible (　　　) we misunderstood what he was saying.
   ① because　　　② that　　　③ what　　　④ whether

🎧 Listening　英文を聞いて理解しよう【知識・技能】【思考力・判断力・表現力】　共通テスト　CD 41

Listen to the English and make the best choice to match the content. (4点)

① Augustus was Roman Emperor for about 40 years.

② Octavian became emperor in B.C. 14.

③ Octavian became Roman Emperor when he was 27 years old.

💬 Interaction　英文を聞いて会話を続けよう【知識・技能】【思考力・判断力・表現力】　スピーキング・トレーナー　CD 42

Listen to the English and respond to the last remark. (7点)

　　［メ モ　　　　　　　　　　　　　　　　　　　　　　　　　　　　　　　　　］

　　アドバイス　legendary animal「伝説上の生き物」

✎ Production (Write)　自分の考えを書いて伝えよう【思考力・判断力・表現力】

Write your answer to the following question. (7点)

　　If you were an emperor of ancient China, when would you change the name of the era?

　　アドバイス　本文中の Emperor Wu の例を参考に，どんなときに変えたいか，また変えたくないのならその理由を答えよう。

------

⑦ Recent era names in Japan / have **signified** a common feeling / shared by Japanese people. // For example, / they remember Heisei / as a peaceful period. // There were no wars in Japan / in the Heisei era. // The Heisei Emperor often went / to World War II **memorial** sites / and **prayed** that the spirits of the war dead / would rest in peace. // This gave Japanese people deep **comfort**. //

⑧ On the day when the era name Reiwa was announced, / the **Prime Minister** expressed his hope / that the new era would lead to a bright future. // He **interpreted** Reiwa / as a time / when people's beautiful hearts and minds would create a new culture. // People in Japan / hold wishes for world peace. // One woman said, / "I hope / that all children can grow strong in peace / in the new era." //

⑨ More than 200 era names have been used / in Japan, / and each era **witnessed** / both good and sad events. // Most of those events / might not be recorded / in history books, / but they surely remain / in our deep memories. // What memory in the new era / will be handed down / to future generations? // (182 words)

🔊 **音読しよう**

スピーキング・トレーナー

Practice 1　スラッシュ位置で文を区切って読んでみよう□
Practice 2　イントネーションに注意して読んでみよう□
TRY!　　　1分50秒以内に本文全体を音読しよう□

📖 **Reading**　本文の内容を読んで理解しよう【知識・技能】【思考力・判断力・表現力】　　共通テスト

Make the correct choice to complete each sentence or answer each question. (各4点)

1. The Heisei Emperor often visited World War II memorial sites to _____.

　① give Japanese people deep comfort

　② pray for the spirits of the war dead

　③ pray for the world's economic growth

　④ take a rest in peaceful environment

2. Which of the following is true about Japanese people in the beginning of a new era? _____

　① They hold wishes for world peace.

　② They hope to be a leader of the world.

　③ They pray that all children grow strong.

　④ They wish to create a new culture.

3. Each of Japan's more than 200 eras _____.

　① has only good memories which remain in our memories

　② has variety of events which are not related to our future generations

　③ includes both good and bad events

　④ recorded all the events in history books

🔍 Vocabulary & Grammar　重要表現や文法事項について理解しよう【知識】　　英検® GTEC®

Make the correct choice to complete each sentence. （各2点）

1.　The agreement between the two companies (　　　　) their continuous expansion in the country.

① agrees　　　　② compiles　　　　③ reveals　　　　④ signifies

2.　(　　　　) for the sake of the world peace.

① Look　　　　② Pray　　　　③ Search　　　　④ Thanks

3.　She's a great (　　　　) to her parents.

① comfort　　　　② feeling　　　　③ kindness　　　　④ luxury

4.　Many people (　　　　) the accident.

① happened　　　　② hit　　　　③ involved　　　　④ witnessed

5.　This is positive proof (　　　　) he is guilty.

① of　　　　② of that　　　　③ that　　　　④ whether

🎧 Listening　英文を聞いて理解しよう【知識・技能】【思考力・判断力・表現力】　共通テスト CD 43

Listen to the English and make the best choice to match the content.（4点）

① In "Reiwa" era, world peace is more important for people than politeness.

② The name "Reiwa" gave many people an impression of peace.

③ The speaker investigated the impression that the name "Reiwa" makes on people.

💬 Interaction　英文を聞いて会話を続けよう【知識・技能】【思考力・判断力・表現力】　スピーキング・トレーナー CD 44

Listen to the English and respond to the last remark.（7点）

［メモ　　　］

アドバイス　2つの時代がどんなところが異なるか考えると，理由を考えやすいでしょう。

✏ Production (Write)　自分の考えを書いて伝えよう【思考力・判断力・表現力】

Write your answer to the following question.（7点）

What is your best memory from the Heisei era?

アドバイス　My best memory from the Heisei era is ... と書き始めるとよいでしょう。理由なども忘れずに書こう。

In English class, / your teacher gave a **worksheet** / to your group. // You are listening / to a group discussing / a student's translation / of a *haiku*. //

Task // **Translate** the *haiku* below / into English. //
Tips //
Translate it / in three lines. // Start each line / with a small letter. //
You don't need / a period / at the end. // Use short and simple words. //
Try not to use / "I" or "you." //
Use **nouns**, / **rather** than **verbs** / or **adjectives**. // If you use verbs, / use them / in the present **tense**. //
Don't worry / about grammar / too much. //
Translation:/ When you eat a **persimmon**, / you can hear / a bell **toll** / at Horyuji. //
    (Satoshi) //
Satoshi: I made my translation / as clear and easy / to **comprehend** / as possible. // What do you think of it, / Kazuki? //
Kazuki: You did a good job, / but I think / this is too long / for a translation / of a *haiku*. // Also, / we should try not to use / "you." // Can't we make it simpler / and make it sound / more like *haiku*? //
Emily: I agree with Kazuki. // In English *haiku*, / we don't have to start / with a capital letter. // We should make it / in three lines. // I think / the first line should be something / like "eat a persimmon." //
Satoshi: Very good, / Emily! // Then, / the second line can be / "and a bell will toll." // The final line can be / "at Horyuji." // Let's put the lines / together! //
    eat a persimmon / and a bell will toll / at Horyuji //   (230 words)

🔊 音読しよう   スピーキング・トレーナー
Practice 1   スラッシュ位置で文を区切って読んでみよう □
Practice 2   イントネーションに注意して読んでみよう □
TRY!   2分20秒以内に本文全体を音読しよう □

📖 **Reading**   本文の内容を読んで理解しよう【知識・技能】【思考力・判断力・表現力】   共通テスト

Make the correct choice to complete each sentence or answer each question. (各6点)

1. Which of the following is **not** true about the rules for translating *haiku* in English?
    ☐
    ① A *haiku* consists of three lines.
    ② A period is not necessary at the end.
    ③ Each line starts with a small letter.
    ④ Only nouns and verbs can be used.

2. ☐ thought that the first translation had room for improvement in terms of length.
    ① Emily   ② Kazuki   ③ Satoshi   ④ The teacher

🔍 Vocabulary & Grammar　重要表現や文法事項について理解しよう【知識】　英検® GTEC®

Make the correct choice to complete each sentence. (各2点)

1. Here are a few (　　　) to make your speech attractive.
   ① moments　　　② occasions　　　③ tips　　　④ understandings

2. Change the (　　　) into the past tense in the following sentences.
   ① adjectives　　　② adverbs　　　③ nouns　　　④ verbs

3. The Abbey bell (　　　) for those killed in the war.
   ① broke　　　② called　　　③ hit　　　④ tolled

4. It took me a while to (　　　) what he was saying.
   ① comprehend　　　② disagree　　　③ emphasize　　　④ resolve

5. He (　　　) the novel from English into Japanese.
   ① divided　　　② prevented　　　③ translated　　　④ turned

6. The movie was exciting (　　　) than educational.
   ① better　　　② less　　　③ more　　　④ rather

7. I called my mother at eleven, (　　　) she was already sleeping.
   ① during　　　② that　　　③ when　　　④ where

8. There is no hope (　　　) the politician will recover from illness.
   ① how　　　② of　　　③ that　　　④ when

🎧 Listening　英文を聞いて理解しよう【知識・技能】【思考力・判断力・表現力】　

Listen to the English and make the best choice to match the content. (各4点)

1. Who taught Ann about the Ryakujin Era?
   ① A university teacher
   ② Dorothy
   ③ Her grandfather
   ④ Satoshi

2. How did Ann know that emperors in the past often changed era names?
   ① Because her grandfather is Japanese.
   ② Because she read it in a book.
   ③ From the Internet.
   ④ Satoshi taught it to her.

3. Which of the following is true about changes of era names?
   ① Emperors after the Meiji era often changed the era name.
   ② Era names were changed only when the emperor changed.
   ③ Era names were never changed after the Meiji era.
   ④ Era names were sometimes changed by good or bad events.

You want / to gather information / about food loss and waste. // You found / a Q&A site. //

Is it true / that there is enough food / to feed all the people / on the earth? //

Answer: / Takehiko Ogawa, / a social studies teacher / at a high school in Japan / since 2001 //
　　It's true / that we can feed everyone / on the earth. // For example, / about 2.6 billion **metric** tons of **cereals** / are produced **annually** / all over the world. // If they were **distributed evenly** / to all of the people / around the world, / each person could have / over 330 kilograms of cereals to eat / in a year. // That is more than double the amount / that a Japanese **consumes** / in a year. //
　　Nevertheless, / it is also true / that more than 820 million people, / or one in nine people / in the world, / are suffering / from **hunger**. // This **implies** / that food is not **equally** available / to everyone. // In fact, / about half the cereals produced worldwide / are consumed / in developed countries, / whose population is less than 20% / of the world population. //
　　Moreover, / the **truth** is / that about one third of the food / produced for human consumption / is lost or wasted / every year. // This amounts to / about 1.3 billion metric tons. // If we save one fourth of the lost or wasted food, / we will save enough food / for all the hungry people / in the world. // (207 words)

🔊 **音読しよう**　　　　　　　　　　　　　　　　　　　　　　　スピーキング・トレーナー

Practice 1　スラッシュ位置で文を区切って読んでみよう ☐
Practice 2　イントネーションに注意して読んでみよう ☐
TRY!　　　　2分以内に本文全体を音読しよう ☐

📖 **Reading**　　本文の内容を読んで理解しよう【知識・技能】【思考力・判断力・表現力】　　共通テスト

Make the correct choice to complete each sentence or answer each question. (各6点)

1. It is true that ☐ .

　① cereals produced in the world are distributed evenly to everyone

　② each person in Japan eats 330 kilograms of cereals in a year

　③ enough cereals for everyone on the planet are produced today

　④ the amount of cereals produced on the earth so far is about 2.6 billion tons

2. Which of the following is true about the hunger problem? ☐

　① About half the cereals produced worldwide are lost or wasted, and this causes worldwide hunger.

　② Cereals are distributed to everybody in the world so the problem of hunger has been solved.

　③ If we save one third of lost or wasted food, we will be able to save all of the hungry people in the world.

　④ One in nine people on earth are suffering from hunger.

🔍 Vocabulary & Grammar　重要表現や文法事項について理解しよう【知識】　　英検® GTEC®

Make the correct choice to complete each sentence. (各2点)

1. The international conference is held (　　　　).
   ① annual　　　② annually　　　③ every　　　④ year

2. Her fine clothes (　　　) that she was rich.
   ① implied　　　② heard　　　③ looked　　　④ told

3. That antique car (　　　　) a huge amount of fuel but has a lot of fans all over the world.
   ① connects　　　② consoles　　　③ consumes　　　④ continues

4. The teacher (　　　　) the handouts for the next examination to the students.
   ① disappeared　　　② disciplined　　　③ discovered　　　④ distributed

5. (　　　　) to music, my brother cleaned his room.
   ① Listen　　　② Listened　　　③ Listening　　　④ To listen

🎧 Listening　英文を聞いて理解しよう【知識・技能】【思考力・判断力・表現力】　共通テスト　CD 46

Listen to the English and make the best choice to match the content. (4点)

① The speaker is interested in food problems.

② The speaker's father has never been to African countries.

③ The speaker's father probably knows much about global food problems.

💬 Interaction　英文を聞いて会話を続けよう【知識・技能】【思考力・判断力・表現力】　スピーキング・トレーナー　CD 47

Listen to the English and respond to the last remark. (7点)

［メモ　　］

アドバイス　最初の発言はあなたの発言です。あなたの誘いに対して相手がどうしてその質問をするのかを考えよう。

💬 Production (Speak)　自分の考えを話して伝えよう【思考力・判断力・表現力】　スピーキング・トレーナー

Speak out your answer to the following question. (7点)

Do you think it is good to eat up all your dinner every day?

アドバイス　なぜそう考えるのかを説明しよう。

The world population / is estimated to reach 9.7 billion / in 2050, / and global food problems / are expected to become / even more serious. //

① Too much food produced / for human beings / is lost or wasted / in the food supply chain. // Food loss occurs / early in the chain / —— before the food even gets / to stores and consumers. // For example, / in developing countries, / farmers lose / a large part of their **crops** / because they don't have / **appropriate storage equipment**. // Food is often eaten / by **bugs** and small **creatures**. // **Furthermore**, / food is sometimes lost / during transportation. // For instance, / food may go bad / if it is **transported** / in trucks without **refrigeration**. //

② On the other hand, / food waste occurs / at the end of the chain / —— in stores, / restaurants / and houses. // Food that is past its best-before date / is **discarded** / at **grocery** stores, / and **uneaten** food is thrown away / at restaurants. // In our home, / **leftover** food goes bad / in the fridge / and is thrown away. //

③ Having recognized the importance / of reducing food loss and waste, / the United Nations is encouraging people / to take action. // As one of the targets / of SDGs, / we need to reduce food waste / by half / and cut down the amount / of food loss / by 2030. // Governments, / organizations / and **individuals** around the world / have begun / to make efforts / to achieve this target. // (218 words)

◀ 音読しよう　　　　　　　　　　　　　　スピーキング・トレーナー
Practice 1 スラッシュ位置で文を区切って読んでみよう☐
Practice 2 イントネーションに注意して読んでみよう☐
TRY!　　　　2分10秒以内に本文全体を音読しよう☐

📖 **Reading** 本文の内容を読んで理解しよう【知識・技能】【思考力・判断力・表現力】　　　共通テスト

Make the correct choice to complete each sentence. (各4点)

1. Food loss occurs ☐ .
   ① at the end of the food supply chain　② early in the food supply chain
   ③ in stores, restaurants and houses　④ only in farms

2. Food waste occurs ☐ .
   ① before the food reaches the consumer
   ② in farms or during transportation
   ③ in stores, restaurants and houses
   ④ only at houses

3. According to the passage, ☐ has recognized the importance of reducing food loss and waste.
   ① individuals around the world　② one of the targets of SDGs
   ③ people who are taking actions　④ the United Nations

🔊 イントネーションを理解して音読することができる。
📖 フードロスとフードウェイストに関する英文を読んで，概要や要点を捉えることができる。
🔍 文脈を理解して適切な語句を用いて英文を完成することができる。
🎧 平易な英語で話される短い英文を聞いて必要な情報を聞き取ることができる。　🗨 食品廃棄について簡単な語句を用いて説明することができる。
✏ 賞味期限について簡単な語句を用いて考えを表現することができる。
oals

🔍 Vocabulary & Grammar　重要表現や文法事項について理解しよう【知識】　英検® GTEC®

Make the correct choice to complete each sentence. (各2点)

1. The new hospital in our city has advanced (　　　　) and facilities, so the number of complicated operations has been increasing.

   ① equipment　　　② equipments　　　③ furniture　　　④ materials

2. The downloaded data should be (　　　　) immediately because it might contain a computer virus.

   ① differed　　　② digested　　　③ discarded　　　④ distributed

3. A: Bob, heat up the (　　　　) for lunch.

   B: OK, mom.

   ① carry-over　　　② hangover　　　③ leftovers　　　④ takeover

4. The milk I bought last Saturday (　　　　). I can't drink it anymore.

   ① went bad　　　② went crazy　　　③ went mad　　　④ went well

5. (　　　　) heard from my friend Emma, I decided to send an e-mail to her.

   ① Had　　　② Have had　　　③ Not have　　　④ Not having

🎧 Listening　英文を聞いて理解しよう【知識・技能】【思考力・判断力・表現力】　共通テスト　CD 48

Listen to the English and make the best choice to match the content. (4点)

　① The farmer couldn't sell all of the vegetables.

　② The farmer had to throw away his products.

　③ The typhoon made the farmer give up growing vegetables.

💬 Interaction　英文を聞いて会話を続けよう【知識・技能】【思考力・判断力・表現力】　スピーキング・トレーナー　CD 49

Listen to the English and respond to the last remark. (7点)

　[メモ　　　　　　　　　　　　　　　　　　　　　　　　　　　　　　　　　　　]

　アドバイス　身の回りで食品廃棄がどんな時に起こるかを想像してみよう。

✏ Production (Write)　自分の考えを書いて伝えよう【思考力・判断力・表現力】

Write your answer to the following question. (7点)

　What do you think about eating food that is past its best-before date?

　アドバイス　賞味期限切れの食べ物に対して普段どういう対応を取っているかを思い出してみよう。

----

④ France was the first country / to make a law / to reduce food waste. // Since 2016, / large supermarkets have been **prohibited** / from throwing away food. // Instead, / they have been **required** / to donate it / or turn it into **compost** / or animal feed. // France has become a leader / in food waste **reduction** / and has inspired / other countries. //

⑤ In the Spanish town of Galdakao, / a community **refrigerator** was placed / on a **sidewalk** / in 2015. // People from **nearby** restaurants and **households** / put their **excess** food and leftovers / into the fridge, / and **whoever** wants them / can take them / for free. // The movement of setting up community refrigerators / has been spreading / to many other countries, / including the U.K., / **Belgium**, / **Argentina** / and **Israel**. //

⑥ October 16 is "World Food Day," / which was established / by the United Nations. // In Japan, / the entire month of October / has been **designated** / as "World Food Day Month." // During this period, / various food events are held / all over Japan. // For example, / in an event / in 2019, / participants were asked / to post recipes / using **unused** food / on social media. // Sponsors of the event / donated 120 yen / per post to a charity / that supported school meals / in Africa. //

(191 words)

🔊 音読しよう

Practice 1　スラッシュ位置で文を区切って読んでみよう □
Practice 2　イントネーションに注意して読んでみよう □
TRY!　　　 1分50秒以内に本文全体を音読しよう □

スピーキング・トレーナー

📖 **Reading**　本文の内容を読んで理解しよう【知識・技能】【思考力・判断力・表現力】　　共通テスト

Make the correct choice to complete each sentence or answer each question. (各4点)

1. Which of the following is true about the law on food waste in France? ☐
   ① It prohibited people from using food to feed animals.
   ② It required large supermarkets not to throw away food.
   ③ It was intended to reduce food waste, but it was ineffective.
   ④ Large supermarkets in France don't have to follow it.

2. A community refrigerator was placed in the Spanish town of Galdakao in 2015 and ☐ .
   ① people have been using it to get foods at reasonable prices
   ② people have been putting foods to turn into compost or animal feed in it
   ③ this idea has been spreading to many other countries
   ④ whoever in need of a refrigerator has been using it

3. ☐ was held in Japan in 2019.
   ① A charity event whose participants donated 120 yen per post
   ② A charity event whose sponsors donated money for school meals in Africa
   ③ A cooking event whose participants' recipes were used
   ④ A cooking event whose visitors brought excess food and leftovers

🔍 Vocabulary & Grammar　重要表現や文法事項について理解しよう【知識】　英検® GTEC®

Make the correct choice to complete each sentence. (各2点)

1. "(　　　　)" is the original word but in English conversation we often use a shortened version of it.

① Air conditioner　② Refrigerator　③ Vacuum cleaner　④ Washing machine

2. [空港で] Could you tell me how much the (　　　) baggage charge is?

① excess　　　② more　　　③ over　　　④ surpassed

3. My mother (　　　) me from playing video games since my test result was terrible.

① proceeded　　② prohibited　　③ promoted　　④ provided

4. The kind lawyer gave me some legal advice (　　　).

① for example　② for free　　③ for fun　　④ for sure

5. There are many kinds of chocolate here. You can take (　　　) you like.

① however　　② wherever　　③ whichever　　④ whoever

🎧 Listening　英文を聞いて理解しよう【知識・技能】【思考力・判断力・表現力】　共通テスト CD 50

Listen to the English and make the best choice to match the content. (4点)

① Students were encouraged to develop their opinions to reduce food waste.

② The teacher posted her idea to reduce food waste on the Internet.

③ The school homepage asked students to give their ideas for it.

💬 Interaction　英文を聞いて会話を続けよう【知識・技能】【思考力・判断力・表現力】　スピーキング・トレーナー CD 51

Listen to the English and respond to the last remark. (7点)

[メ モ　　　　　　　　　　　　　　　　　　　　　　　　　　　　　　　　　　]

アドバイス　本文中に書かれた情報を参考にして答えよう。

✏️ Production (Write)　自分の考えを書いて伝えよう【思考力・判断力・表現力】

Write your answer to the following question. (7点)

If you had a chance, what kind of charity food event would you want to participate in?

アドバイス　聞いたことがあるイベントでもよいし，自分でイベントの主旨を考えてもよいでしょう。

----

⑦ Another way / to **tackle** the problem of food loss and waste / is to use technology. // Recently, / various food-sharing apps have been developed / and are receiving special attention. // These apps help match people / who don't want to discard food / with people who need it. //

⑧ Some apps connect a person / to another person. // When you have more food / than you can eat / in your home, / you can use these apps / to find someone / to share it with. // Other apps link **retailers** / to **shoppers**. // A supermarket can post **discount** information / about **unsold** food. // Shoppers can **purchase** / this unsold food cheaply / with the app / and come to the supermarket later / to pick it up. // There are also some apps / that connect stores / to charity organizations. // When a restaurant has a **surplus** of food / that will **spoil** soon, / it can donate the food. // These apps help reduce / food loss and waste / at every point / along the food supply chain. //

⑨ Food loss and waste / is a global issue. // Everyone in the world / has to understand / the causes of this problem / and make an effort / to solve it. // When these efforts bear fruit, / we will finally have a world / free of hunger. // (195 words)

◀)) **音読しよう**　　　　　　　　　　　　　　　　　　　スピーキング・トレーナー

Practice 1   スラッシュ位置で文を区切って読んでみよう ☐
Practice 2   イントネーションに注意して読んでみよう ☐
TRY! 　　　 2分以内に本文全体を音読しよう ☐

📖 **Reading**   本文の内容を読んで理解しよう【知識・技能】【思考力・判断力・表現力】   共通テスト

Make the correct choice to complete each sentence or answer each question. (各4点)

1. According to paragraph 7, food-sharing apps help ☐ .

  ① connect stores and restaurants

  ② link restaurants to customers

  ③ match people who don't want to discard food with people who need it

  ④ match supermarkets with charity organizations

2. At which point of the food supply chain do these apps contribute to reducing food loss and waste? ☐

  ① At an early point of it.   ② At every point along it.

  ③ At some point along it.   ④ At the end of it.

3. Which of the following best summarizes Lesson 6? ☐

  ① Food loss and waste has been solved through the efforts of everyone in the world.

  ② Food loss and waste is a problem that involves everyone, and efforts are being made to solve it.

  ③ Governments must make laws to solve food loss and waste problem.

  ④ The use of technology is one of the ways to solve food loss and waste.

🔍 Vocabulary & Grammar　重要表現や文法事項について理解しよう【知識】 　英検◉ GTEC◉

Make the correct choice to complete each sentence.（各2点）

1. Ted is a team leader.　He always (　　　　) a difficult task with his positive attitude.

   ① approves　　　② makes　　　　③ tackles　　　　④ works

2. The ticket shop often sells (　　　　) event tickets on the Internet.

   ① unfair　　　② unhappy　　　③ unimportant　　　④ unsold

3. He has decided to (　　　　) the latest computers and printers to use in his office.

   ① publish　　　② punish　　　③ purchase　　　④ pursue

4. I wonder if my efforts will bear (　　　　).

   ① children　　　② fruit　　　③ interest　　　④ vegetable

5. Don't worry.　I'll advise you (　　　　) necessary.

   ① however　　　② whichever　　　③ whenever　　　④ wherever

🎧 Listening　英文を聞いて理解しよう【知識・技能】【思考力・判断力・表現力】 　共通テスト CD 52

Listen to the English and make the best choice to match the content.（4点）

   ① All customers can get discount information from the store.

   ② The store provides discount information three times a week.

   ③ Users of the store's app receive the discount information.

💬 Interaction　英文を聞いて会話を続けよう【知識・技能】【思考力・判断力・表現力】 スピーキング・トレーナー CD 53

Listen to the English and respond to the last remark.（7点）

〔メモ　　　　　　　　　　　　　　　　　　　　　　　　　　　　　　　　　　〕

アドバイス　会話の場面を想像しよう。

✏️ Production（Write）　自分の考えを書いて伝えよう【思考力・判断力・表現力】

Write your answer to the following question.（7点）

Give an example of food loss or food waste problem that may occur around you.

アドバイス　コンビニでの弁当廃棄など，身近で食品に関する「もったいないな」と思うことを思い出してみよう。

You **responded** / to an **online questionnaire** / made by your **Assistant** Language Teacher. // After all the students answered, / a **slide** with a graph was generated. //

Introduction //
I am studying / about food loss and waste / in daily life. // I would like to ask you / to fill out this questionnaire. // It only takes / about five minutes. // The results will be used / for my study, / and I will give a research presentation / at a later date. // Thank you / in **advance** / for your help. //
Questionnaire / about food loss and waste //
Q: Are you or your family members doing something / to reduce food waste / in your home? // Please check all the actions / that are true for your family, / and then check who is/are doing them. // (You may choose / more than one **option**. //)
1. ☐ ___ make/makes a shopping list before going shopping at the supermarket. //
2. ☐ ___ often go/goes to the supermarket and buy/buys less food each time. //
3. ☐ ___ don't/doesn't pay too much attention to best-before dates. //
4. ☐ ___ store/stores leftovers in the refrigerator instead of throwing them away. //
5. ☐ ___ don't/doesn't cook more food than family members can eat. //
6. ☐ ___ make/makes **pickles** from unused vegetables. //
(☐ I ☐ mother ☐ father ☐ brother(s) ☐ sister(s) ☐ other [   ])

(125 words)

🔊 音読しよう　　　　　　　　　　　　　　　　　　　スピーキング・トレーナー
Practice 1　スラッシュ位置で文を区切って読んでみよう ☐
Practice 2　イントネーションに注意して読んでみよう ☐
TRY!　　　1分20秒以内に本文全体を音読しよう ☐

📖 **Reading**　本文の内容を読んで理解しよう【知識・技能】【思考力・判断力・表現力】　　共通テスト

Answer each question. (各6点)

1. How long does it take to fill out this questionnaire? ☐
   ① About fifteen minutes.　　　　② About fifty minutes.
   ③ About five hours.　　　　　　④ About five minutes.

2. According to the result of the questionnaire, who is most conscious of food loss and waste issue? ☐
   ① Brother(s)　　② Father　　③ Mother　　④ Sister(s)

🔍 Vocabulary & Grammar   重要表現や文法事項について理解しよう【知識】   英検® GTEC®

Make the correct choice to complete each sentence. (各2点)

1. Please answer the (   ) before you leave the theater.
   ① questionnaire   ② research   ③ survey   ④ test

2. We offer an (   ) air ticket booking service. You can get tickets at reasonable prices from the Internet.
   ① offline   ② ongoing   ③ online   ④ onsite

3. This car is standard white, but there are eight color (   ) to choose from.
   ① operations   ② opinions   ③ opponents   ④ options

4. The customer service department has to (   ) customer requests right away.
   ① replace with   ② rescue from   ③ respect for   ④ respond to

5. Monthly rent is required to be paid (   ).
   ① in advance   ② in fact   ③ in turn   ④ in vain

6. (   ) too much last night, my father has a stomachache.
   ① Ate   ② Eating   ③ Had eaten   ④ Having eaten

7. (   ) I hear this song, I remember my great-grandmother.
   ① Whatever   ② Whenever   ③ Whichever   ④ Whoever

8. (   ) reading the book, she returned it to the library.
   ① Finished   ② Had finished   ③ Have finished   ④ Having finished

🎧 Listening   英文を聞いて理解しよう【知識・技能】【思考力・判断力・表現力】   共通テスト CD 54

Listen to the English and make the best choice to match the content. (各4点)

1. What does OzHarvest Market sell?
   ① Food after the best-before date
   ② Food brought by an NPO
   ③ Food waste
   ④ Food we have to eat as soon as possible

2. What do shoppers have to do before shopping?
   ① Ask some questions.   ② Discuss with other shoppers.
   ③ Find a store clerk.   ④ Wait for someone.

3. Which of the following is true about OzHarvest Market?
   ① It pays salaries to the full-time sales staff.
   ② Most of the clerks there don't know about the food there at all.
   ③ Shoppers can receive food for free.
   ④ Shoppers have to eat food immediately in the store.

61

Koji and an Assistant Language Teacher are talking / about a map / of the world. //

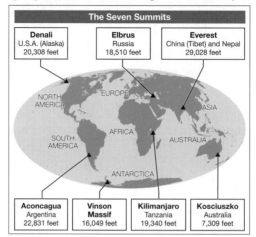

The Seven Summits

| **Denali** U.S.A. (Alaska) 20,308 feet | **Elbrus** Russia 18,510 feet | **Everest** China (Tibet) and Nepal 29,028 feet |

NORTH AMERICA　EUROPE　ASIA　AFRICA　AUSTRALIA　SOUTH AMERICA　ANTARCTICA

| **Aconcagua** Argentina 22,831 feet | **Vinson Massif** 16,049 feet | **Kilimanjaro** Tanzania 19,340 feet | **Kosciuszko** Australia 7,309 feet |

Koji: What's that? //

ALT: Hi, / Koji! // It's a map / that shows the highest mountain / on each **continent**. //

Koji: Wow, / how interesting! // I know / you like climbing mountains. // Where would you like to go? //

ALT: I want / to climb Mt. Everest / someday. // Do you know / about the **Explorer's Grand Slam**? // It is the **accomplishment** / of climbing the highest mountain / on each continent, / including Mt. Everest, / and going to the North and South **Poles**. //

Koji: Oh, / wow! // That must be / very hard / to do. // How many people / have done it? //

ALT: About 50 people / have done it / so far! // And a female Japanese university student / became the youngest person / in the world / to complete this great achievement / in 2017. // (125 words)

🔊 音読しよう 　　　　　　　　　　　　　　　　スピーキング・トレーナー

Practice 1 　スラッシュ位置で文を区切って読んでみよう ☐
Practice 2 　音の変化に注意して読んでみよう ☐
TRY! 　　　１分20秒以内に本文全体を音読しよう ☐

📖 **Reading** 　本文の内容を読んで理解しよう【知識・技能】【思考力・判断力・表現力】 　　共通テスト

Make the correct choice to complete each sentence. (各6点)

1. The ALT has a map that shows ☐ .
   ① the area where she is from 　　　② the highest mountain in the world
   ③ the highest mountain on each continent
   ④ the route to the top of Mr. Everest

2. One **opinion** about the Explorer's Grand Slam is that " ☐ ."
   ① about 50 people have accomplished it
   ② going to the North Pole is one of the goals of it
   ③ it is very hard to achieve
   ④ the youngest achiever of it is a Japanese

🔍 Vocabulary & Grammar　重要表現や文法事項について理解しよう【知識】　　英検。 GTEC。

Make the correct choice to complete each sentence. (各 2 点)

1. Jessica's family is proud of her academic (　　　　).
   ① accomplishments　② efforts　　　　　③ powers　　　　　④ training

2. The canal separates the African (　　　　) from Asia.
   ① commerce　　　　② consumer　　　　③ continent　　　　④ country

3. The South (　　　　) is much colder than the North (　　　　).
   ① area　　　　　　② point　　　　　　③ pole　　　　　　④ spot

4. How many points has your team got (　　　　)?
   ① by far　　　　　② for now　　　　　③ so far　　　　　④ too far

5. If I (　　　　) enough money, I could buy the latest smartphone.
   ① have　　　　　　② had　　　　　　③ had had　　　　　④ having

🎧 Listening　英文を聞いて理解しよう【知識・技能】【思考力・判断力・表現力】　　共通テスト　CD 55

Listen to the English and make the best choice to match the content. (4 点)

① Listeners can find out the number of Japanese who reached the top of Mt. Everest.

② The speaker is a Japanese person who has climbed Mt. Everest once.

③ The table includes some data over the last twelve years.

💬 Interaction　英文を聞いて会話を続けよう【知識・技能】【思考力・判断力・表現力】　スピーキング・トレーナー　CD 56

Listen to the English and respond to the last remark. (7 点)

[メモ　　　　　　　　　　　　　　　　　　　　　　　　　　　　　　　　　　　　　]

アドバイス　補足的な情報を知っていれば加えよう。other than ... 「…以外で」。

💬 Production (Speak)　自分の考えを話して伝えよう【思考力・判断力・表現力】　スピーキング・トレーナー

Speak out your answer to the following question. (7 点)

Do you have any goals for the near future?

アドバイス　遠い将来的な目標ではなく，近い将来に達成したい目標を考えよう。

Marin Minamiya completed a remarkable achievement. // What **motivated** her? // What made her reach / for her dream? //

① "**Strive** toward your goal / with passion. // Nothing is stronger / than our will. // A person's potential is / truly **infinite**," / says Marin Minamiya. // She completed the Explorer's Grand Slam / when she was 20 years old. //

② Marin was born / in Tokyo / on December 20, / 1996. // Since her father worked / for a **trading** company, / her family moved / to various places, / including **Malaysia**, / **mainland** China and Hong Kong. // She lived / outside Japan / from a young age, / and it was difficult / for her / to **identify** herself / as Japanese. // When she was 13 years old / in Hong Kong, / she got an **opportunity** / to climb some mountains / with her classmates. // This became a turning point / in her life. // Each climb taught her / something new, / and **afterward** / she felt as if she had escaped / from all stress and **anxiety**. //

③ One day, / Marin went **trekking** / in Nepal, / and she saw Mt. Everest / for the first time. // Everything about the **magnificent** mountain was / eye-opening for her. // The experience inspired her / greatly / and provided her / with courage, / **faith** / and power. // She said, / "I knew / that I would come back / to the great Everest / one day. // I wanted / to **explore** myself / and learn the purpose / of my **existence**." // (211 words)

🔊 **音読しよう**　　　　　　　　　　　　　　　　スピーキング・トレーナー

Practice 1　スラッシュ位置で文を区切って読んでみよう ☐
Practice 2　音の変化に注意して読んでみよう ☐
TRY!　　　　2分10秒以内に本文全体を音読しよう ☐

📖 **Reading**　本文の内容を読んで理解しよう【知識・技能】【思考力・判断力・表現力】　　共通テスト

Make the correct choice to complete each sentence or answer each question. (各4点)

1. Marin Minamiya accomplished the Explorer's Grand Slam at the age of ☐ .
   ① 13　　　　　　② 18　　　　　　③ 19　　　　　　④ 20

2. Which of the following places has she never lived in? ☐
   ① China　　　　② Hong Kong　　③ Malaysia　　④ Nepal

3. When Marin saw Mt. Everest, she ☐ .
   ① could finally identify herself as Japanese
   ② knew that climbing would take away her stress and anxiety
   ③ thought she would never see that view again
   ④ wanted to know what she was living for

🔍 Vocabulary & Grammar　重要表現や文法事項について理解しよう【知識】　　英検 ® GTEC®

Make the correct choice to complete each sentence. (各2点)

1. How can we (　　　　) the students in the classroom?
   ① brighten　　　　② express　　　　③ glow　　　　④ motivate

2. Everything you (　　　　) for as a team seems to be going the right way.
   ① head　　　　② look　　　　③ strive　　　　④ try

3. He (　　　　) the coat as his brother's.
   ① accepted　　　　② agreed　　　　③ explained　　　　④ identified

4. He went first to Fukuoka, and (　　　　) to Osaka to study philosophy.
   ① after　　　　② afterward　　　　③ forward　　　　④ onward

5. He talked (　　　　) he knew her secrets.
   ① as for　　　　② as if　　　　③ as of　　　　④ as to

🎧 Listening　英文を聞いて理解しよう【知識・技能】【思考力・判断力・表現力】　共通テスト　CD 57

Listen to the English and make the best choice to match the content. (4点)

① The speaker and her father lived separately for a long time.

② The speaker's father still lives abroad away from her.

③ The speaker's father has never lived in Japan.

💬 Interaction　英文を聞いて会話を続けよう【知識・技能】【思考力・判断力・表現力】　スピーキング・トレーナー　CD 58

Listen to the English and respond to the last remark. (7点)

　　［メ モ　　］

　　アドバイス　遠足などを思い出してみよう。また，会話を続けることを意識しよう。

✏ Production（Write）　自分の考えを書いて伝えよう【思考力・判断力・表現力】

Write your answer to the following question. (7点)

　　Have you had any eye-opening experiences?

　　アドバイス　それをきっかけに変わったことなどを付け加えよう。

----

④　When Marin was 17, / she started / preparing for climbing Mt. Everest. // She told her father / about her **ambition**. // However, / he said, / "I won't support you / **financially**. // This is your project / and you're old enough / to figure out / what to do / on your own." // Since she had no **assistance**, / she had to **request** support / from companies / while studying and training. // Some people told her / she would not **succeed**. // However, / a strong will **arose** in her / and defeated such **negative** words. // She thought, / "If I give up, / I will be a person / who never tried anything." // Luckily, / she received **financial** support / from many **firms**. //

⑤　As a first step, / Marin climbed Mt. Aconcagua / in her last year of high school. // In the following year, / she climbed Mt. Kilimanjaro, / Mont Blanc / and Mt. Manaslu. // Finally, / the day came / when her dream was realized. // In May 2016, / at the age of 19, / she was standing on Everest / above the clouds, / above all her difficulties. //

⑥　Marin's dream kept growing / as she **conquered** more mountains. // Never did she stop / challenging herself, / even though some people said / her challenges were impossible. // She set her sights / on the Seven Summits / and, eventually, / on the Explorer's Grand Slam. //　(198 words)

🔊 **音読しよう**

スピーキング・トレーナー

Practice 1　スラッシュ位置で文を区切って読んでみよう ☐
Practice 2　音の変化に注意して読んでみよう ☐
TRY!　　　　2分以内に本文全体を音読しよう ☐

📖 **Reading**　本文の内容を読んで理解しよう【知識・技能】【思考力・判断力・表現力】　　共通テスト

Make the correct choice to complete each sentence or answer each question. (各4点)

1.　Marin's father refused to support her financially as ☐.

① he thought that she would not succeed

② she was old enough to figure out what to do on her own

③ studying was what he thought she needed to do most

④ the family couldn't afford it

2.　When did she realize her dream? ☐

① When she climbed Mt. Manaslu.

② When she was in the last year of high school.

③ When she was 17.

④ When she was 19.

3.　After Marin conquered Mt. Everest, she ☐.

① kept growing taller

② set her sights on the Explorer's Grand Slam

③ was proud of defeating those who said her challenges were impossible

④ stopped challenging herself

🔊 音の変化を理解して音読することができる。
📖 南谷真鈴さんに関する英文を読んで，概要や要点を捉えることができる。
🔍 文脈を理解して適切な語句を用いて英文を完成することができる。
🎧 平易な英語で話される短い英文を聞いて必要な情報を聞き取ることができる。　　💬 成功者について簡単な語句を用いて説明することができる。
✏️ 登山について簡単な語句を用いて想像して考えを表現することができる。

Goals

🔍 Vocabulary & Grammar　重要表現や文法事項について理解しよう【知識】　　英検® GTEC®

Make the correct choice to complete each sentence. (各2点)

1. He lacked (　　　　) and couldn't compete with the others.
   ① ambition　　　　② despair　　　　③ freedom　　　　④ problem

2. The country was in a bad situation (　　　　).
   ① emotionally　　② financially　　③ originally　　④ physically

3. She hopes to (　　　) her fear of speaking in public.
   ① conquer　　　　② escape　　　　③ research　　　　④ struggle

4. My cat is smart enough to (　　　) where the treat is hidden.
   ① bring out　　　② figure out　　　③ push out　　　④ run out

5. Not until this morning (　　　) that it had snowed.
   ① did I realize　　② didn't I realize　　③ I did realize　　④ I didn't realize

🎧 Listening　英文を聞いて理解しよう【知識・技能】【思考力・判断力・表現力】　　共通テスト　CD 59

Listen to the English and make the best choice to match the content. (4点)

① The speaker needed nine months to prepare financially for his project.

② The speaker is now climbing Mt. Kilimanjaro with his project members.

③ The speaker won't climb Mt. Kilimanjaro due to the lack of money.

💬 Interaction　英文を聞いて会話を続けよう【知識・技能】【思考力・判断力・表現力】　スピーキング・トレーナー　CD 60

Listen to the English and respond to the last remark. (7点)

［メモ　　］

アドバイス　有名ではない身近な人でもよいでしょう。思いつかない場合は相手に質問をしてみよう。

✏️ Production (Write)　自分の考えを書いて伝えよう【思考力・判断力・表現力】

Write your answer to the following question. (7点)

How do you think you would feel if you were on top of Mt. Everest?

アドバイス　状況を想像してみよう。

⑦　Marin has **accomplished** the Explorer's Grand Slam, / **proving** that there is nothing / we cannot do / if we keep trying. // "Am I what I want to be?" // This question made her set out / for the mountains. // Climbing mountains / and keeping her motivation / **enabled** her / to prove herself / and conquer her weaknesses. // They taught her / that anything could be **attained**; / any summit could be reached, / no matter how high / it might be. //

⑧　Marin is now preparing / for her next adventure. // She hopes to **sail** / to various countries / with a **human-powered** yacht / and talk about life and the future / with children there. // Marin says, / "To live is to **weave** your **tapestry** / with different **patterns**. // The patterns and colors in our tapestries / are determined / by how we live. // We need / to ask ourselves / what we want to do / in order to make / our own special tapestries." //

⑨　This is Marin's message / to us all: / "Even though your steps may seem small, / they will surely combine / to become a great **leap** / to make your future / better. // Believe that you are going to make it / through everything / you are doing. // There is nothing / as strong as your passions / to make your dreams come true." //

(197 words)

🔊 **音読しよう**

スピーキング・トレーナー

Practice 1　スラッシュ位置で文を区切って読んでみよう ☐
Practice 2　音の変化に注意して読んでみよう ☐
TRY!　　　2分以内に本文全体を音読しよう ☐

📖 **Reading**　本文の内容を読んで理解しよう【知識・技能】【思考力・判断力・表現力】　　共通テスト

Make the correct choice to complete each sentence or answer each question. (各4点)

1.　What Marin proved is that ☐ .

① all things are achievable no matter how difficult they are

② climbing mountains is necessary to overcome people's weaknesses

③ the Explorer's Grand Slam is not very difficult to accomplish

④ we cannot get anything without keeping trying

2.　Which of the following opinions would Marin agree with? ☐

① All should try to actually weave the tapestry themselves.

② Each person should live the life he or she wants to live.

③ Instead of asking ourselves, we should act first.

④ We should live our lives while respecting the opinions of others.

3.　What is the most important thing to make your dreams come true? ☐

① Adventures are.　② Passions are.　　③ Small steps are.　④ Tapestries are.

🔍 Vocabulary & Grammar 重要表現や文法事項について理解しよう【知識】 英検® GTEC®

Make the correct choice to complete each sentence. （各2点）

1. Have you (   ) everything you have to do today?

   ① abandoned　　　② accomplished　　　③ acquired　　　④ applied

2. He designed an experiment to (   ) his theory.

   ① improve　　　② proof　　　③ prove　　　④ provide

3. That's one small step for a man, one giant (   ) for humankind.

   ① footprint　　　② harvest　　　③ leap　　　④ record

4. Toyotomi Hideyoshi (   ) Kyoto after hearing the death of his lord, Nobunaga.

   ① came down on　　　② made up to　　　③ pull out of　　　④ set out for

5. (   ) dream that I would marry her.

   ① Did I little　　　② I little did　　　③ Little did I　　　④ Little I did

🎧 Listening 英文を聞いて理解しよう【知識・技能】【思考力・判断力・表現力】 共通テスト CD 61

Listen to the English and make the best choice to match the content. （4点）

① He played the piano in the international competition.

② The International competition was held in Switzerland in October.

③ He is going to study music in the college in Europe.

💬 Interaction 英文を聞いて会話を続けよう【知識・技能】【思考力・判断力・表現力】 スピーキング・トレーナー CD 62

Listen to the English and respond to the last remark. （7点）

[メモ　　　　　　　　　　　　　　　　　　　　　　　　　　　　　　　　　　]

アドバイス　相手はどんなことに悩んでいるのでしょうか。あなたなりにアドバイスをしてあげよう。

✏️ Production（Write） 自分の考えを書いて伝えよう【思考力・判断力・表現力】

Write your answer to the following question. （7点）

What are your strengths and weaknesses?

アドバイス　長所と短所は表裏一体です。indecisive「優柔不断な」↔ careful「慎重な」，thoughtful「思慮深い」

In class, / students are sharing / their plans / for the future / while showing **charts** / about their goals. // You are listening / to a student's presentation / about her goals / and action plans. //

Terms	Goals	**Detailed** actions to take
By the end of high school	· Improve my grades · Play in the **regional** tennis tournament	· Study hard in every class · Pass quizzes and tests · Attend extra lessons · Practice tennis hard
By the end of college	· **Broaden** my **perspectives**	· Study abroad · Do volunteer work · Join events in my community
By the age of 30	· Work for a trading company	· Study economics · Take language lessons

　　Hi! // Here are my future goals / and the detailed actions / I will take / to achieve them. // During high school, / I will improve my **academic** abilities. // I study hard / in every class / and at home. // I'm in the tennis club / and our team has a goal / of **participating** in the regional tournament. // All the members of my club / practice very hard. // During college, / I will broaden my perspectives / and meet many new people / from around the world. // By the time I'm 30 years old, / I **definitely** want / to work for a trading company. // To realize my dream, / I plan to study economics / and gain a good **command** / of several languages. // Thank you / for listening. //

(142 words)

🔊 音読しよう

Practice 1 スラッシュ位置で文を区切って読んでみよう ☐

Practice 2 音の変化に注意して読んでみよう ☐

TRY!　　1分30秒以内に本文全体を音読しよう ☐

スピーキング・トレーナー

📖 **Reading** 本文の内容を読んで理解しよう【知識・技能】【思考力・判断力・表現力】　　共通テスト

Make the correct choice to complete each sentence or answer each question. (各4点)

1. What club does the student belong to? ☐

　　① badminton　　　② gymnastic　　　③ soccer　　　④ tennis

2. She wants to work for a trading company by the time she is ☐ years old.

　　① 13　　　　　　② 20　　　　　　③ 30　　　　　　④ 40

3. According to the presentation, what does she need to realize her dream? ☐

　　① Economic knowledge and language skills.

　　② Experience of studying abroad.

　　③ Having many friends around the world.

　　④ Toughness to practice tennis hard.

Vocabulary & Grammar 重要表現や文法事項について理解しよう【知識】 英検® GTEC®

Make the correct choice to complete each sentence. (各2点)

1. The company is located at four different areas, each directed by a (　　) manager.
   ① radical ② rational ③ regional ④ responsible

2. He is currently in his third (　　) as a politician.
   ① grade ② span ③ term ④ time

3. Opening an online store can be a good way to (　　) your business.
   ① broaden ② open ③ prolong ④ suspend

4. The tour guide gave us tips to see the castle from a historical (　　).
   ① experience ② perspective ③ point ④ view

5. Nealy 100 players (　　) in the game.
   ① attended ② participated ③ reached ④ took

6. The foreigners with only a poor (　　) of English didn't know what to do.
   ① collect ② command ③ copper ④ corridor

7. I wish Wataru (　　) with us now.
   ① be ② is ③ had ④ were

8. Hardly (　　) the door when my mother knocked on it.
   ① closed ② had I closed ③ I closed ④ I had closed

Listening 英文を聞いて理解しよう【知識・技能】【思考力・判断力・表現力】 共通テスト CD 63

Listen to the English and make the best choice to match the content. (各4点)

1. When will the speaker start helping his uncle's restaurant?
   ① Around 30.
   ② After graduating from technical school.
   ③ After moving to Nagoya.
   ④ By the age of 35.

2. What does the speaker want to learn about in France?
   ① Basic cooking skills ② French skills
   ③ Local culture ④ Restaurant management skills

3. Which of the following is true?
   ① The speaker wants to open his restaurant soon after returning to Japan.
   ② The speaker wants to run his own restaurant by the age of 40.
   ③ The speaker will go to the technical school in Nagano.
   ④ The speaker's uncle has a restaurant but doesn't cook there.

You have bought a **brand-new smartwatch**. // You are reading / the user **manual** / to find out / how to **charge** the watch. //

STEP 1 /

Connect the USB **plug** / of the battery charger / to the **port** of an AC **adapter**. //

STEP 2 /

Place the watch / on the charger. // Make sure / that it touches the charging **pins**. // If the watch is **correctly** connected, / the charging **icon** (⚡) will appear / on the watch screen. // If you cannot see the icon, / you will need / to check the contact / between the charger and the watch. //

STEP 3 /

When the watch fully charges, / "100%" will be **displayed** / on the watch screen / and the watch will automatically stop charging. // It takes about one hour / for the watch to charge / fully. //

Notes: /

The proper temperature range for charging is / between 10℃ and 30℃. // The watch may not charge properly / below or above these temperatures. //

The charger has been developed / **specifically** for this product. // The use of an **unauthorized** charger / may damage the watch. //

Do not try / to change the battery / in the watch. // The battery is built-in / and should be replaced / only at an **authorized** service center. //　(186 words)

🔊 **音読しよう**　　　　　　　　　　　　　　　　　　　　スピーキング・トレーナー

Practice 1　スラッシュ位置で文を区切って読んでみよう ☐

Practice 2　音の変化に注意して読んでみよう ☐

TRY!　　　　1分50秒以内に本文全体を音読しよう ☐

📖 **Reading**　本文の内容を読んで理解しよう【知識・技能】【思考力・判断力・表現力】　　　共通テスト

Make the correct choice to complete each sentence or answer each question. (各6点)

1. To charge the watch, what should you do after placing it on the charger? ☐

① You should confirm if the watch touches the charging pins.

② You should confirm that the charging icon disappears.

③ You should connect the watch to the port of AC adapter.

④ You should prepare the battery charger.

2. In order to change the battery in the watch, you should get it replaced ☐ .

① at an authorized service center

② at the manufacturer

③ at the shop you bought it

④ by yourself

🔍 Vocabulary & Grammar　重要表現や文法事項について理解しよう【知識】　　英検® GTEC®

Make the correct choice to complete each sentence. (各2点)

1. He went out in his (　　　) car this morning. He seemed so happy.

　① alternative　　　② brand-new　　　③ original　　　④ recently

2. The "L" sound is difficult for many non-native speakers to pronounce. I would like

　to pronounce it (　　　).

　① correctly　　　② fully　　　③ lovely　　　④ quickly

3. (　　　) access to our website must be blocked.

　① Authorized　　　② Inefficient　　　③ Unauthorized　　　④ Unimportant

4. She had (　　　) selected her dress to please the audience of the award ceremony.

　① absolutely　　　② literally　　　③ specifically　　　④ visually

5. (　　　) speaking, Japanese people work too much.

　① Generally　　　② Regularly　　　③ Ridiculously　　　④ Strangely

🎧 Listening　英文を聞いて理解しよう【知識・技能】【思考力・判断力・表現力】　　共通テスト　CD 64

Listen to the English and make the best choice to match the content. (4点)

　① The listener is told to see step 5 to solve the problem.

　② The listener seemed to read page 4 at first.

　③ The speaker is being taught how to use a device.

💬 Interaction　英文を聞いて会話を続けよう【知識・技能】【思考力・判断力・表現力】　スピーキング・トレーナー　CD 65

Listen to the English and respond to the last remark. (7点)

〔メ モ　　　　　　　　　　　　　　　　　　　　　　　　　　　　　　〕

　アドバイス　どう使いたいかなどの補足情報を加えよう。

💬 Production (Speak)　自分の考えを話して伝えよう【思考力・判断力・表現力】　スピーキング・トレーナー

Speak out your answer to the following question. (7点)

　Do you have any battery-powered items?

　アドバイス　身の回りにすぐに見つかるでしょう。

Batteries, / particularly rechargeable ones, / are essential / in our daily lives. // What **technological** advances have been made / in the history of batteries? //

① Batteries are now a large part / of our lives. // They are at the heart of everyday **mobile** devices, / such as smartphones, / **tablets** / and **laptop** computers. // **Hybrid** and **electric** cars would not **exist** / without powerful batteries. // **Innovations** in batteries / have had a great **impact** / on the success of new technologies. //

② Good rechargeable batteries are necessary / in order to make **efficient** use / of renewable energy sources, / such as sunlight and wind. // These energy sources depend highly / on the weather, / and they may not be able / to produce enough electricity / when it is most needed. // This is when batteries come into play: / they store electricity / until it is needed. //

③ Rechargeable batteries / can contribute to saving the environment. // **Currently**, / single-use **primary** batteries **occupy** / most of the market. // They are used / only once / and are then thrown away. // Billions of such batteries become waste / every year, / and most of them end up in landfills. // In contrast, / rechargeable batteries can be reused / many times, / and this **lessens** / the waste problem of primary batteries. // Rechargeable batteries are becoming more important / as a **means** / to achieve a sustainable, / greener future. // (203 words)

◀)) 音読しよう　　　　　　　　　　　　　　　　　　スピーキング・トレーナー
Practice 1　スラッシュ位置で文を区切って読んでみよう ☐
Practice 2　音の変化に注意して読んでみよう ☐
TRY!　　　　2分以内に本文全体を音読しよう ☐

📖 **Reading**　本文の内容を読んで理解しよう【知識・技能】【思考力・判断力・表現力】　　共通テスト

Make the correct choice to complete each sentence or answer each question. (各4点)

1.　We can say that batteries ☐ .

　① can be used only once, so it lessens the waste problem

　② cannot be used to store the power by renewable energy sources

　③ have made our convenient society possible

　④ should be used less in order to reduce the waste

2.　According to paragraph 2, what is the disadvantage of using renewable energy sources? ☐

　① They can still cause pollution.　② They can't always generate sufficient power.

　③ They often have lower power.　④ The technology can be expensive.

3.　Which of the following are true about single-use primary batteries? (Choose two options. The order does not matter.) ☐ ・ ☐

　① They are reused many times.

　② They are used only once and most of them end up in landfills.

　③ They can contribute to saving the environment.

　④ They occupy most of the market.

🔍 Vocabulary & Grammar　　重要表現や文法事項について理解しよう【知識】　　　　英検® GTEC®

Make the correct choice to complete each sentence. (各2点)

1. Weather can have an impact (　　　　) your mood and behavior.

　① by　　　　　　　② in　　　　　　　③ on　　　　　　　④ with

2. The newspaper says Japan's automakers need to adopt more (　　　　) production plans than before.

　① arrogant　　　　② competent　　　③ delight　　　　④ efficient

3. The coffee shop will (　　　　) the first floor of this new building.

　① locate　　　　　② occupy　　　　　③ place　　　　　④ set

4. Walking as a (　　　　) of transportation will promote human health.

　① mean　　　　　② means　　　　　③ methods　　　　④ ways

5. (　　　　) a little more care, you wouldn't have made such a terrible mistake.

　① But for　　　　② With　　　　　③ Within　　　　④ Without

🎧 Listening　　英文を聞いて理解しよう【知識・技能】【思考力・判断力・表現力】　　共通テスト CD 66

Listen to the English and make the best choice to match the content. (4点)

　① The speaker has to find a battery charger.

　② The speaker wants to buy a red smartphone.

　③ The speaker's smartphone is not working.

💬 Interaction　　英文を聞いて会話を続けよう【知識・技能】【思考力・判断力・表現力】　スピーキング・トレーナー　CD 67

Listen to the English and respond to the last remark. (7点)

　[メモ　　　　　　　　　　　　　　　　　　　　　　　　　　　　　　　　　　　　　]

　アドバイス　dispose of ... 「…を捨てる」　　collection day「収集日」

✎ Production（Write）　　自分の考えを書いて伝えよう【思考力・判断力・表現力】

Write your answer to the following question. (7点)

　Do you know any renewable energy sources?

　アドバイス　再生可能エネルギーにはどんな種類があるか，調べてみよう。

....

....

④ What does a typical battery **consist** of? // It has two **electrical** ends / and a **chemical** between them. // These parts **react** with each other / inside the battery. // As a result, / electricity is produced. // Many different chemicals can be used / in batteries / and, generally speaking, / they determine a battery's power. //

⑤ The word "battery" / goes back to the 18th century. // It was first used / by Benjamin Franklin / of the U.S. // He called a device / he invented / an "electrical battery." // It could only store electricity. // In 1800, / Alessandro Volta of Italy / developed a "true" battery. // He used **copper**, / **zinc** / and salt water / in his device, / and his battery could produce electricity / **chemically**. // However, / it couldn't **recharge** / for reuse. //

⑥ The earliest rechargeable battery was / the **lead-acid** battery. // It was invented / in 1859. // This type is still widely used / in cars. // In 1899, / **nickel-cadmium** batteries were created, / and they were a top choice / for use in portable devices / for many years. // In the 1990s, / nickel-**metal hydride** batteries took over. // They had a longer life. // They were also less **harmful** / to the environment. // Later, / as people wanted smaller and better batteries, / **lithium-ion** batteries were developed. // (188 words)

🔊 音読しよう

Practice 1 スラッシュ位置で文を区切って読んでみよう ☐
Practice 2 音の変化に注意して読んでみよう ☐
TRY! 1分50秒以内に本文全体を音読しよう ☐

スピーキング・トレーナー

📖 **Reading** 本文の内容を読んで理解しよう【知識・技能】【思考力・判断力・表現力】 共通テスト

Answer each question. (1. 完答8点, 2. 4点)

1. Complete the table below by filling in each blank (A) ~ (K).

1700s	The word "battery" was first used by Benjamin Franklin. He called his device "electrical battery." It could only (A) electricity.
1800s	The "true" battery was developed by Alessandro Volta. It could (B) electricity chemically but couldn't (C) for reuse.
1859	The earliest (D) battery, the (E) battery, was invented. This type is still widely used in (F).
1899	The (G) battery was created. They were used in (H) for many years.
1990s	The (I) battery took over. They had a (J) life and were less (K) to the environment.

① cars　　　　　② harmful　　　　③ lead-acid　　　④ longer
⑤ nickel-cadmium　⑥ nickel-metal hydride　　⑦ portable devices
⑧ produce　　　⑨ recharge　　　⑩ rechargeable　⑪ store

2. After nickel-metal hydride batteries, ☐ were developed.
　① dry cells　　　　　　　② lead-acid batteries
　③ lithium-ion batteries　　④ nickel-cadmium batteries

🔊 音の変化を理解して音読することができる。
📖 電池の歴史と仕組みに関する英文を読んで，概要や要点を捉えることができる。
🔍 文脈を理解して適切な語句を用いて英文を完成することができる。
🎧 平易な英語で話される短い英文を聞いて必要な情報を聞き取ることができる。　🔊 電気自動車について簡単な語句を用いて考えを表現することができる。
✏ モバイルバッテリーについて簡単な語句を用いて考えを表現することができる。

oals

🔍 Vocabulary & Grammar　重要表現や文法事項について理解しよう【知識】　英検® GTEC®

Make the correct choice to complete each sentence.（各2点）

1. The manual explains that this chair (　　　) of five parts.
   ① considers　② consists　③ combines　④ completes

2. According to the study, the new plastic bottle is not (　　　) to the environment.
   ① faithful　② grateful　③ harmful　④ successful

3. Susan will take (　　　) the position of general manager at the company.
   ① about　② away　③ down　④ over

4. The forests in this area have been destroyed by (　　　) rain.
   ① acid　② gentle　③ light　④ moderate

5. (　　　) speaking, his presentation was boring.
   ① Frankly　② Logically　③ Originally　④ Technically

🎧 Listening　英文を聞いて理解しよう【知識・技能】【思考力・判断力・表現力】　共通テスト CD 68

Listen to the English and make the best choice to match the content.（4点）

① The speaker asked someone to change his car battery.
② The speaker drove his car to the supermarket to buy the car battery.
③ The speaker replaced his car battery with the old one.

💬 Interaction　英文を聞いて会話を続けよう【知識・技能】【思考力・判断力・表現力】　スピーキング・トレーナー　CD 69

Listen to the English and respond to the last remark.（7点）

［メモ　　　］

アドバイス　それぞれのメリットとデメリットを考えてみよう。

✏ Production（Write）　自分の考えを書いて伝えよう【思考力・判断力・表現力】

Write your answer to the following question.（7点）

Do you think mobile batteries are necessary for your daily life?

アドバイス　外出先で充電の必要性があるかどうか，考えてみよう。

⑦ The 2019 Nobel Prize in **Chemistry** / went to Japanese scientist / Akira Yoshino. // He shared the prize / with John B. Goodenough / of the U.S. // and Britain's Stanley Whittingham. // They were recognized / for their work / on the lithium-ion battery / (LIB). // Yoshino made the battery safe / and **commercially usable** / for the first time. //

⑧ The lithium-based battery was invented / by Whittingham / in the 1970s. // However, / his battery did not last / very long. // To make matters worse, / it also had a serious safety concern, / as it could catch fire and **explode**. // In the 1980s, / a more powerful type was developed / by Goodenough. // He used lithium-**cobalt oxide** / on one end of the battery. // Some years later, / Yoshino made a step / further. // He **adopted** Goodenough's idea, / but he used carbon / on the other end. // This cleared the way / for a safe, / **stable** / and practical LIB. //

⑨ The LIB is one of the most common batteries / today. // Its evolution does not stop, / and many important discoveries / continue to be made. // Lithium-ion technology is / still full of **unknowns** / and **possibilities**. // Yoshino believes / that the LIB can play a central role / in creating a society / without fossil fuels. // LIB technology is bringing / great power to people / around the world. // (198 words)

🔊 **音読しよう**

スピーキング・トレーナー

Practice 1 スラッシュ位置で文を区切って読んでみよう ☐
Practice 2 音の変化に注意して読んでみよう ☐
TRY!   2分以内に本文全体を音読しよう ☐

📖 **Reading**   本文の内容を読んで理解しよう【知識・技能】【思考力・判断力・表現力】   共通テスト

Make the correct choice to complete each sentence or answer each question.

(1. 3点, 2. 完答6点, 3. 3点)

1. Akira Yoshino won the 2019 Nobel Prize in Chemistry for his work on ☐ .

① inventing the lithium-ion battery though it had a short life

② inventing the lithium-ion battery which had a safety problem

③ making the lithium-ion battery powerful

④ making the lithium-ion battery safe and commercially usable

2. Complete the table below by filling in each blank (A) ~ (E).

Whittingham	He (A) the lithium-ion battery (LIB) in the 1970s. It didn't (B) very long and had a serious problem.
Goodenough	He developed a more (C) type with lithium-cobalt oxide in 1980s.
Yoshino	He (D) Goodenough's idea. He used carbon and made a safe, stable and (E) LIB.

[① adopted ② invented ③ last ④ powerful ⑤ practical]

■» 音の変化を理解して音読することができる。
□ リチウムイオン電池に関する英文を読んで，概要や要点を捉えることができる。
♀ 文脈を理解して適切な語句を用いて英文を完成することができる。
♀ 平易な英語で話される短い英文を聞いて必要な情報を聞き取ることができる。
♀ ノーベル賞について簡単な語句を用いて説明することができる。　　　　♂ 発明について簡単な語句を用いて考えを表現することができる。
oals

3. Which of the following is **not** true about the LIB? ☐

① It can play a central role in creating a society without fossil fuels.

② It is still uncommon but it can possibly change our society.

③ Its evolution does not stop, and many important discoveries continue to be made.

④ Its technology is bringing great power to people around the world.

🔍 Vocabulary & Grammar　重要表現や文法事項について理解しよう【知識】　英検® GTEC®

Make the correct choice to complete each sentence. (各2点)

1. Shanghai is known as a (　　　　) important city.
   ① commercially　　② illegally　　③ mentally　　④ positively

2. Eddie had to (　　　) a positive attitude to continue playing on the team.
   ① act　　② adapt　　③ adopt　　④ adore

3. Claire is always very patient but she (　　　) with anger this morning. I want to know what happened to her.
   ① expected　　② expired　　③ explained　　④ exploded

4. Unfortunately, there is no (　　　) that he will win in the final.
   ① possibility　　② reason　　③ use　　④ way

5. (　　　), I am scared of darkness because I believe in ghosts.
   ① All things to considered　　　　② Generally speaking
   ③ So to speak　　　　④ To tell the truth

🎧 Listening　英文を聞いて理解しよう【知識・技能】【思考力・判断力・表現力】　共通テスト　CD 70

Listen to the English and make the best choice to match the content. (4点)

① The doctor invented great technology before.

② The doctor hasn't worked for Oxford University.

③ The speaker had been a professor at Oxford University.

💬 Interaction　英文を聞いて会話を続けよう【知識・技能】【思考力・判断力・表現力】　スピーキング・トレーナー　CD 71

Listen to the English and respond to the last remark. (7点)

[メモ　　　　　　　　　　　　　　　　　　　　　　　　　　　　　　　　　]

アドバイス　化学賞に限らず，ノーベル平和賞や物理学賞の受賞者でもよい。その人の功績についても簡単に答えよう。

✏️ Production（Write）　自分の考えを書いて伝えよう【思考力・判断力・表現力】

Write your answer to the following question. (7点)

What do you think is the most important invention in human history?

アドバイス　ここ最近の製品のほうが説明しやすいでしょう。

You are listening / to Akira Yoshino speaking / shortly after the announcement / of his Nobel Prize / in Chemistry. //

Q1) How did you feel / when you heard / you were awarded / the prize? //

I couldn't believe the news, / and it didn't feel real / at first. // On the phone, / I had an interview / in English. // Actually, / I felt **uneasy** / about it / because I thought my English interview / would be **broadcast** / around the world. //

Q2) How can the lithium-ion battery help / a society / based on renewable energy? //

I believe / lithium-ion batteries in electric cars / can help greatly. // Our future society needs / a better power storage system. // If electric cars become **widespread**, / they can **compose** / a huge power storage system. // That will **stimulate** / the use of solar and wind power. //

Q3) What message do you have / for young people / who are interested / in science? //

You should look for and **nourish** / a seed of interest. // In my case, / it was a book / about **candles**. // When I read it, / I thought / chemistry was fascinating. // That experience / has led to my work / on the lithium-ion battery. // When you get interested / in something / and work toward it, / you will become better / at it. //

(190 words)

◀)) 音読しよう スピーキング・トレーナー

Practice 1 スラッシュ位置で文を区切って読んでみよう ☐
Practice 2 音の変化に注意して読んでみよう ☐
TRY! 1分50秒以内に本文全体を音読しよう ☐

📖 **Reading** 本文の内容を読んで理解しよう【知識・技能】【思考力・判断力・表現力】 共通テスト

Make the correct choice to complete each sentence or answer each question. (各4点)

1. Yoshino felt uneasy about an interview in English because he thought ⬚.
   ① he didn't deserve the prize
   ② his interview would be broadcast around the world
   ③ the interview was too short to express his feelings
   ④ the news of winning the Nobel Prize was a fake

2. According to Yoshino, what does our future society need? ⬚
   ① A better power storage system.
   ② Lithium-ion batteries for electric cars.
   ③ Lithium-ion batteries for portable devices.
   ④ More eco-friendly electric cars.

3. What was the beginning of Yoshino's interest in chemistry? ⬚
   ① Changing batteries in his watch. ② Nourishing seeds in the ground.
   ③ Reading a book about candles. ④ Studying science at school.

🔍 Vocabulary & Grammar 　重要表現や文法事項について理解しよう【知識】　英検® GTEC®

Make the correct choice to complete each sentence. (各2点)

1. My grandfather had an operation yesterday and our family spent an (　　　) day.
   ① uneasy　　　　② unfair　　　　③ unlucky　　　　④ unreal

2. ZYX TV will (　　　) a news program from next Saturday.
   ① advertise　　　② broadcast　　　③ contribute　　　④ perform

3. The thunderstorms hit this area and caused (　　　) power outages last night.
   ① broad　　　　② deep　　　　③ pandemic　　　④ widespread

4. The smell of curry (　　　) my appetite.
   ① excites　　　　② installs　　　③ motivates　　　④ stimulates

5. Female mammals produce milk to (　　　) their babies.
   ① cultivate　　　② nourish　　　③ provide　　　④ sustain

6. Weather (　　　), we will go to the amusement park tomorrow.
   ① permitted　　　② permits　　　③ permitting　　　④ permission

7. (　　　) her looks, she seemed to be exhausted.
   ① Judged from　　② Judging for　　③ Judging from　　④ Judging with

8. (　　　) his effort, he wouldn't have succeeded.
   ① But　　　　② Not　　　　③ With　　　　④ Without

🎧 Listening 　英文を聞いて理解しよう【知識・技能】【思考力・判断力・表現力】　共通テスト CD 72

Listen to the English and make the best choice to match the content. (各4点)

1. What did the Japanese company do in 1991?
   ① It developed the lithium-ion polymer battery.
   ② It invented the lithium-ion battery.
   ③ It released the lithium-ion battery.　　④ It sold the lithium-ion polymer battery.

2. Which of the following is true?
   ① The LIB was developed following the lithium-ion polymer battery.
   ② The lithium-ion polymer battery produces electricity differently from the LIB.
   ③ The lithium-ion polymer battery uses a sheet of iron to protect the inside.
   ④ There is no liquid chemical in the lithium-ion polymer battery.

3. From the information you heard, you can say that lithium-ion polymer batteries
   [　　　].
   ① are environmentally friendly as they last longer without recharging
   ② are much more powerful than lithium-ion batteries
   ③ have been used for most of portable devices in the world
   ④ have the advantage of being light and small

You are reading / a blog post / about a famous tree / in Hokkaido / which was very popular / among tourists. //

I have to tell you / a very disappointing thing. // **Unfortunately**, / a famous tree on a farm / in Biei, / Hokkaido, / was finally cut down / by the **landowner**. // This tree, / **leaning** far to one side / in the middle of a field, / **resembled** a **philosopher** / in deep thought. // That is why / it came to be called / the "Philosophy Tree." //

Occasionally, / the owner could not work / on his farm / because of tourists / blocking the road / with their parked cars. // More and more tourists entered / his **private** land / to get the best shots / on their smartphones, / and they damaged his crops. // They ignored **warning** signs / saying, / "PRIVATE PROPERTY: / NO ENTRY." // The signs were written / not only in Japanese and English / but also in Chinese and Korean. //

I, / and maybe other people / in Japan, / too, / felt a sense of **crisis**. // On **behalf** of the **bloggers** / in Japan, / I wrote about it / on this blog. // In the end, / the worst result has come about / and I am shocked. // I am afraid / that similar **incidents** with tourists / may happen / in other popular areas / in the future. // What can we do / to prevent this? // What **measures** / should we take? // (208 words)

🔊 **音読しよう**

スピーキング・トレーナー

Practice 1   スラッシュ位置で文を区切って読んでみよう ☐
Practice 2   音の変化に注意して読んでみよう ☐
TRY!   2分以内に本文全体を音読しよう ☐

📖 **Reading**   本文の内容を読んで理解しよう【知識・技能】【思考力・判断力・表現力】   共通テスト

Make the correct choice to complete each sentence or answer each question. (各4点)

1. Why was the tree called the "Philosophy Tree"? ☐
    ① Biei was known for a place of the philosophy study.
    ② It resembled a philosopher in deep thought.
    ③ It was planted by a famous philosopher.
    ④ The landowner studied philosophy.

2. Why was the tree cut down? ☐
    ① Because the owner wanted more space to grow his crops.
    ② Because the tree became so big that the sunlight was blocked.
    ③ Because tourists' cars sometimes prevented the owner from working on his farm.
    ④ Because tourists refused to pay entry fees.

3. The writer of the blog ☐.
    ① is accusing the tourists of invading the private property
    ② is blaming the landowner who cut down the tree
    ③ is promoting tourism to Biei
    ④ is raising the alarm as similar incidents may happen in other tourist sites

🔍 Vocabulary & Grammar　重要表現や文法事項について理解しよう【知識】　英検® GTEC®

Make the correct choice to complete each sentence. (各2点)

1. (　　　　), there was nothing to quicken the healing of his illness.
   ① Fortunately　　② Occasionally　　③ Personally　　④ Unfortunately

2. Almost a half of the voters currently (　　　　) toward the youngest candidate.
   ① bend　　② fascinate　　③ lean　　④ tend

3. That mountain is said to (　　　) a human nose.
   ① equal　　② look　　③ resemble　　④ similar

4. (　　　　) of all the A-bomb survivors, the woman spoke out at the UN headquarters.
   ① By means　　② For the purpose　　③ In spite　　④ On behalf

5. This is the house which your grandfather lived (　　　　).
   ① by　　② for　　③ in　　④ on

🎧 Listening　英文を聞いて理解しよう【知識・技能】【思考力・判断力・表現力】　共通テスト CD 73

Listen to the English and make the best choice to match the content. (4点)

① The speaker is taking pictures for his blog post.
② The speaker visited popular photo spots abroad.
③ The speaker will use some pictures on his blog post.

💬 Interaction　英文を聞いて会話を続けよう【知識・技能】【思考力・判断力・表現力】　スピーキング・トレーナー CD 74

Listen to the English and respond to the last remark. (7点)

[メモ　　　　　　　　　　　　　　　　　　　　　　　　　　　　　　　　　　　]

アドバイス　一般的にはその状況は好まれないので，自分だったらどう対応するかを考えよう。

💬 Production (Speak)　自分の考えを話して伝えよう【思考力・判断力・表現力】　スピーキング・トレーナー

Speak out your answer to the following question. (7点)

Do you know any other case of tourists causing trouble to tourist sites? What do you think about it?

アドバイス　知っていることがなくても，本文の内容を参考にしながら，そのような問題に対して自分の意見を述べよう。

Do you want / to travel abroad? // With a **restriction** on non-essential travel / and complete **lockdown** / in some countries, / we were able to witness / what could happen / to the world. //

① Recently, / **tourism** has gone through some **decline** / due to **infectious** diseases / and natural disasters. // In fact, / it is still fresh / in our memory / that the number of tourists decreased **drastically** / in 2020 / due to the influence of COVID-19. // However, / do you remember / that tourists were visiting various spots / in large numbers / at one time? //

② **Overtourism** quickly became / one of the most serious social problems / in the modern age of travel. // More and more people visited sightseeing places, / thanks to cheaper air **fares**, / rising incomes / and the power of social media. // These places were no longer able / to **cope** with their own popularity. // In the past few years, / a number of **destinations** have raised the **alarm** / over this situation. //

③ In 2018, / the Oxford Dictionary chose "overtourism" / as one of its Words of the Year. // The World Tourism Organization defined it / as "the negative impact / that tourism has / on a destination." // An excess of tourist **crowds** impacted / the local people's quality of life. // **Excessive** crowds **hindered** the experiences / of the tourists themselves. // Many places / **dependent** on money from tourism wondered / if they could maintain a good environment / not only for travelers / but also for their own **residents**. // (224 words)

🔊 **音読しよう**

Practice 1　スラッシュ位置で文を区切って読んでみよう ☐

Practice 2　音の変化に注意して読んでみよう ☐

TRY!　　　2分10秒以内に本文全体を音読しよう ☐

スピーキング・トレーナー

📖 **Reading**　本文の内容を読んで理解しよう【知識・技能】【思考力・判断力・表現力】　共通テスト

Make the correct choice to complete each sentence or answer each question. (各4点)

1. ☐ is the cause of the drastic decrease in the number of tourists.
   ① Overtourism
   ② The COVID-19 pandemic
   ③ The Olympic games
   ④ The spread of social media

2. Which of the following is **not** true about the overtourism? ☐
   ① Cheaper air fares, rising incomes and the power of social media contributed to it.
   ② It became a serious social problem quickly.
   ③ It ruined historical buildings and sites all around the world.
   ④ There were many tourist destinations that did not consider it a good thing.

3. The definition of "overtourism" is ☐ .
   ① the negative impact that tourism has on a destination
   ② the new way of traveling that people go over and over
   ③ the positive economic impact that tourism has
   ④ the time that the excessive tourism is over

🔍 Vocabulary & Grammar　重要表現や文法事項について理解しよう【知識】　英検® GTEC®

Make the correct choice to complete each sentence. (各2点)

1. How much is the *Shinkansen* (　　　　) from Kyoto to Tokyo?

   ① cost　　　　　② fare　　　　　③ fee　　　　　④ price

2. The strength of the Tokugawa shogunate began to (　　　) gradually in the middle of 19th century.

   ① decline　　　　② drop　　　　　③ fall　　　　　④ slow

3. Ear buds can (　　　) your ability to hear.

   ① bother　　　　② cut　　　　　③ hinder　　　　④ reveal

4. (　　　　), whaling was an important industry in the United States.

   ① At one time　　② In that case　　③ On earth　　④ To be honest

5. It was surprising (　　　) he won the tournament.

   ① that　　　　　② that to　　　　③ to　　　　　④ which

🎧 Listening　英文を聞いて理解しよう【知識・技能】【思考力・判断力・表現力】　共通テスト CD 75

Listen to the English and make the best choice to match the content. (4点)

① About ten hundred people a day came to the temple before.

② The number of visitors to this temple has decreased significantly.

③ The number of visitors now is about ten times as large as before.

💬 Interaction　英文を聞いて会話を続けよう【知識・技能】【思考力・判断力・表現力】　スピーキング・トレーナー CD 76

Listen to the English and respond to the last remark. (7点)

[メモ　　　　　　　　　　　　　　　　　　　　　　　　　　　　　　　　　　　　　]

アドバイス　国内に限りません。理由も付け加えよう。

✍ Production (Write)　自分の考えを書いて伝えよう【思考力・判断力・表現力】

Write your answer to the following question. (7点)

What would you do at home if you had to stay home during a lockdown?

アドバイス　まとまった時間があるとするなら，家で何をしたいか考えよう。

----

④ At one time, / overtourism was making **headlines** / all over the world. // In Barcelona, / residents protested against many problems / caused by having too many tourists. // In Paris, / workers at the Louvre Museum / went on **strike** over dangerous conditions / resulting from having too many visitors. // In Venice, / residents tried hard / to get **cruise** ships **banned** / from **docking** there. // On Mt. Everest, / some **climbers** have died of **altitude sickness** / because of the **delays** / caused by too many climbers. //

⑤ How about in Japan? // The number of tourists / coming to this country / was once increasing rapidly. // **Inbound** tourism contributed greatly / to the Japanese economy. // Having too many visitors, / however, / can lead to many problems, / such as noise, / litter / and traffic **congestion**. // It can cause great **inconvenience** / to local residents. // It may even spoil the **attraction** / of the sightseeing spot itself. //

⑥ In Kyoto, / people were feeling the negative impacts / of overtourism. // For example, / they had trouble boarding the buses / by which they **commute**. // One of the local residents expressed his mixed feelings: / "Many locals depend on tourism, / so I'm not saying we don't need tourists. // But / we do see / its negative impacts." // Even Japanese tourists avoided visiting Kyoto / because of overtourism. // (195 words)

🔊 **音読しよう**　　　　　　　　　　　　　　　　　　スピーキング・トレーナー

Practice 1　スラッシュ位置で文を区切って読んでみよう☐
Practice 2　音の変化に注意して読んでみよう☐
TRY!　　　　2分以内に本文全体を音読しよう☐

📖 **Reading**　本文の内容を読んで理解しよう【知識・技能】【思考力・判断力・表現力】　　　共通テスト

Answer each question. (各4点)

1. Which of the following is **not** mentioned as an example of overtourism? ☐
   ① Climbers left large amounts of trash and waste on a mountain.
   ② Having too many visitors caused dangerous conditions at a museum.
   ③ So many tourists visited a town that the residents protested against them.
   ④ Too many climbers led to several deaths from altitude sickness.

2. Inbound tourism in Japan contributed greatly to ☐ .
   ① bringing people to villages with small population
   ② the Japanese economy
   ③ those who study foreign language
   ④ widening the understanding of Japanese culture

3. Which of the following is an example of the problems caused by overtourism in Kyoto? ☐
   ① Japanese people avoided living in Kyoto.
   ② Residents in Kyoto had trouble commuting.
   ③ Stores, restaurants and hotels had a labor shortage problem.
   ④ The local economy has become dependent on tourism.

🔊 音の変化を理解して音読することができる。
📖 オーバーツーリズムに関する英文を読んで，概要や要点を捉えることができる。
🔍 文脈を理解して適切な語句を用いて英文を完成することができる。
🎧 平易な英語で話される短い英文を聞いて必要な情報を聞き取ることができる。　🗨 旅行経験について簡単な語句を用いて説明することができる。
✏️ 行列について簡単な語句を用いて考えを表現することができる。
oals

🔍 Vocabulary & Grammar　重要表現や文法事項について理解しよう【知識】　英検® GTEC®

Make the correct choice to complete each sentence. (各2点)

1. Guns are (　　　) in many countries.
   ① banned　　　　② blocked　　　　③ prevented　　　　④ stopped

2. He (　　　) from Shiga to Osaka every day.
   ① commutes　　　② goes　　　　　③ needs　　　　　④ takes

3. Positive consequences will (　　　) from positive actions.
   ① bear　　　　　② bring　　　　　③ carry　　　　　④ result

4. Try shopping in the morning to avoid the (　　　).
   ① calculation　　② collaboration　　③ combination　　④ congestion

5. It is wonderful to have someone on (　　　) you can rely when you need.
   ① that　　　　　② who　　　　　　③ whom　　　　　④ whose

🎧 Listening　英文を聞いて理解しよう【知識・技能】【思考力・判断力・表現力】　共通テスト　CD 77

Listen to the English and make the best choice to match the content. (4点)

① The speaker isn't satisfied with the guesthouse next door.

② The speaker owns a guesthouse next to his house.

③ The speaker will make a claim to his noisy guests.

💬 Interaction　英文を聞いて会話を続けよう【知識・技能】【思考力・判断力・表現力】　スピーキング・トレーナー　CD 78

Listen to the English and respond to the remarks. (7点)

［メモ　　　　　　　　　　　　　　　　　　　　　　　　　　　　　　　　　　　　　］

アドバイス　2つ質問がされるので，そのどちらにも答えよう。

✏️ Production（Write）　自分の考えを書いて伝えよう【思考力・判断力・表現力】

Write your answer to the following question. (7点)

Have you ever waited in a long line? How did it make you feel?

アドバイス　長い行列に並んだ経験を思い出してみよう。

----

⑦ Now is the time / when we should reflect on / what it actually means / to travel. // Imagine / that you are a resident / of a famous tourist destination. // Do you think / people in your town want / to welcome more tourists / from abroad? // Do you think / foreign tourists / who visit your town / will come back again / in the future? //

⑧ **Professor** Harold Goodwin, / who wrote ***Responsible*** *Tourism*, / **remarked**, / "Tourism is like a fire / — you can use it / to cook your food / or it can burn your house down." // Responsible tourism is about making places better / for people to live in / and better for people to visit. // It **demands** responsibility / for achieving sustainable development. //

⑨ How can we achieve responsible tourism / to overcome the problems of overtourism? // There is no single perfect solution / to these problems. // There are, / however, / many ways to reduce crowding / and protect the environment. // It is by taking a more responsible approach / to tourism / that we can **maximize** the positive effects / and **minimize** the negative ones. // We all live / on this beautiful planet / and we are in the same boat. // Traveling should be a **beneficial** experience. // It is up to us / to make sure / it stays that way. //　(197 words)

🔊 **音読しよう**　　　　　　　　　　　　　　　　　　　スピーキング・トレーナー

Practice 1　スラッシュ位置で文を区切って読んでみよう☐
Practice 2　音の変化に注意して読んでみよう☐
TRY!　　　2分以内に本文全体を音読しよう☐

📖 **Reading**　本文の内容を読んで理解しよう【知識・技能】【思考力・判断力・表現力】　　共通テスト

Make the correct choice to complete each sentence. (各4点)

1. You are asked ☐ as a resident of a famous tourist destination.

① when you should reflect on what it actually means to travel

② whether or not you can welcome tourists from abroad

③ whether or not you want to go to other tourist spots

④ why you want to come back to your city

2. Professor Harold Goodwin uses fire as a metaphor for tourism as ☐.

① it can bring us both good and bad results

② it can destroy everything of local residents' properties

③ it can represent our passion for journey to the unknown world

④ it can satisfy traveler's mind with great experiences

3. The author says "we are in the same boat" in order to state that ☐.

① the sea route should be used as a means of transportation

② we all have a duty to make efforts to solve the problem

③ we are a large group of people in a small space

④ we should find the perfect solution to the problem

◀) 音の変化を理解して音読することができる。
📖 新しい旅行様式に関する英文を読んで，概要や要点を捉えることができる。
🔍 文脈を理解して適切な語句を用いて英文を完成することができる。
🎧 平易な英語で話される短い英文を聞いて必要な情報を聞き取ることができる。
🗣 人助けの経験について簡単な語句を用いて説明することができる。　　　　　　✍ 観光地を簡単な語句を用いて紹介することができる。
oals

🔍 Vocabulary & Grammar　重要表現や文法事項について理解しよう【知識】　英検® GTEC®

Make the correct choice to complete each sentence. (各2点)

1. The spilled oil from the tanker was (　　　　) for the deaths of countless marine animals.

   ① available　　　② inevitable　　　③ portable　　　④ responsible

2. My supervisor called Mr. Greenwood and (　　　　) further details.

   ① commanded　　② demanded　　　③ proposed　　　④ wished

3. In order to (　　　　) expenditures, Sean planned to camp out during the tour.

   ① maximize　　　② meet　　　　　③ minimize　　　④ mobilized

4. The roles of bees in nature is (　　　　) for our environment.

   ① artificial　　　② beneficial　　　③ economical　　　④ partial

5. It was not until Mr. Doi taught me (　　　　) I found a clear understanding of mathematics.

   ① about　　　　　② of　　　　　　③ that　　　　　④ what

🎧 Listening　英文を聞いて理解しよう【知識・技能】【思考力・判断力・表現力】　共通テスト　CD 79

Listen to the English and make the best choice to match the content. (4点)

　① The speaker thinks airline tickets for international flights are cheap in summer.

　② Companies need to change the fare for international flights in winter.

　③ If we reduce inbound tourists, airline tickets will be less expensive.

💬 Interaction　英文を聞いて会話を続けよう【知識・技能】【思考力・判断力・表現力】　スピーキング・トレーナー　CD 80

Listen to the English and respond to the last remark. (7点)

［メ モ　　　　　　　　　　　　　　　　　　　　　　　　　　　　　　　　　　　　　　　 ］

　アドバイス　経験がない場合でも，会話を続けるための努力をしよう。

✏️ Production (Write)　自分の考えを書いて伝えよう【思考力・判断力・表現力】

Write your answer to the following question. (7点)

　　Introduce one place that is not famous as tourist spot but is attractive to visit.

　アドバイス　身近な隠れた観光スポットを紹介しよう。

In your class, / you are listening / to a discussion / of the following **statement**: / "In order to prevent overtourism, / people should not post pictures / of their trips / on social media." //

Teacher: As we have learned, / overtourism has become a **crucial** problem / in many places. // When people make a decision / about where to visit and when, / they depend greatly on the information / they see / on social media. // So / for today's discussion, / let's talk about the statement, / "In order to prevent overtourism, / people should not post pictures / of their trips / on social media." // What's your opinion, / Satoshi? //

Satoshi: **Frankly**, / I disagree / with this statement. // Many people want / to travel for the purpose / of taking great pictures / and showing them online. // I think / it's a good thing. // If you don't get hundreds of likes / on your posts, / is it even **worth** going? // If you don't have / any good pictures / to post on social media, / will you still go traveling? // I wouldn't. // How about you, / Emily? //

Emily: Well, / I'm afraid / that traveling has become a photo contest / for many tourists. // **Wherever** I travel, / I see the growing **trend** of / "doing it for social media." // It's all about who can get the best shots, / and it's all evaluated / by the number of likes and followers / you have. // So / I agree / with this statement. // Now, / it's your turn, / Mika. //

Mika: My idea is different / from Emily's. // I believe / that social media can contribute / to helping with "**undertourism**." / That is the movement / for attracting people / to less-visited places / that need more attention. // **Plus**, / I think / social media are not the only reason / for overtourism. // In **conclusion**, / I don't agree / with this statement. // (270 words)

🔊 音読しよう

スピーキング・トレーナー

Practice 1 スラッシュ位置で文を区切って読んでみよう ☐
Practice 2 音の変化に注意して読んでみよう ☐
TRY! 2分40秒以内に本文全体を音読しよう ☐

📖 **Reading** 本文の内容を読んで理解しよう【知識・技能】【思考力・判断力・表現力】 共通テスト

Answer each question. (各6点)

1. Which of the following is **not** true about the contents of the discussion? ☐
   ① Emily thinks posting photos of trips is good for preventing overtourism.
   ② Mika believes social media can contribute to tourism in a good way, too.
   ③ People depend greatly on the information they see on social media.
   ④ Satoshi thinks the purpose of traveling for many people is to take great pictures and show them online.

2. Who agreed with the statement "In order to prevent overtourism, people should not post pictures of their trips on social media."? ☐
   ① All of them did.   ② Emily did.   ③ Mika did.   ④ Satoshi did.

🔍 Vocabulary & Grammar　重要表現や文法事項について理解しよう【知識】　英検® GTEC®

Make the correct choice to complete each sentence. (各2点)

1. Vitamins and minerals are (　　　) to a healthy diet.
   ① controversial　　② crucial　　③ potential　　④ racial

2. She had never heard any student speak so (　　　) to the Principal.
   ① frankly　　② perfectly　　③ quickly　　④ truly

3. His book published in the 19th century, is still (　　　) reading.
   ① no use of　　② used to　　③ worth　　④ worthy

4. The puppy follows me (　　　) I go.
   ① however　　② whenever　　③ wherever　　④ whoever

5. The (　　　) he made was simple and honest, and somehow it made us feel better.
   ① agreement　　② government　　③ payment　　④ statement

6. (　　　), I appreciate the time and efforts of all the people who gathered here today.
   ① As a result　　② Briefly explain　　③ In conclusion　　④ To summarize

7. It will concern all your friends, people (　　　) you have close relationships.
   ① by whom　　② for whom　　③ with whom　　④ who

8. It was a little boy (　　　) found the dinosaur fossil.
   ① having　　② that　　③ to have　　④ which

🎧 Listening　英文を聞いて理解しよう【知識・技能】【思考力・判断力・表現力】　共通テスト　CD 81

Listen to the English and make the best choice to match the content. (各4点)

1. Which of the following is probably true about the listeners?
   ① They don't know where Boracay is.　② They have visited the Philippines.
   ③ They were born in Boracay.　④ They are working for a travel agency.

2. How long was Boracay closed to tourists?
   ① After the autumn of 2018　② Between 2012 and 2018
   ③ For a year　④ For six months

3. Which of the following is true about Boracay?
   ① Hotels and restaurants there caused serious pollution.
   ② It used to receive up to 6,400 tourists a day.
   ③ The Philippine government chose it as the best island in the world.
   ④ The underground water system began to be built after its reopening.

I am sitting / in an **overstuffed** chair / in the **lobby** / of The **Dominion** Imperial International Hotel. // No kidding, / that's really the name. // My friend Wendy **dragged** me here / to meet a guy, / but he doesn't know it. // In fact, / he's never heard of Wendy. // But that doesn't stop her / from being in love with him. // Well, / maybe not in love. // I think / love is for people / you've at least met. // Wendy has never met Craig the Cat. // That's the name of the guy. // At least / that's his stage name. // He's a rock star / who's been famous / for over six months. // Even *my* parents have heard of him. //

Wendy is here / to get Craig the Cat's **autograph** / on his latest album. // She constantly talks about Craig the Cat. // But it was like discussing something / that was going on / in another time **frame**, / on another continent. // I didn't mind. // It was nicely, safely **unreal**. // Until Craig the Cat came to town / today. //

Wendy looks at her watch. // "He's showered / and is relaxing now. // He's feeling rested, / **triumphant**, / and **receptive**." //

"Receptive to what?" //

"To meeting us. // To autographing *my* album." //

"How are you going to accomplish that? // You don't actually know / that he's staying at this hotel, / and even if he is, / you don't know his room number." //

Wendy stands up. // "Don't be so negative, / Rosalind. // Come," / she says. //

I follow her / to one of those telephones / that connect the **caller** to hotel rooms. // She **dials** a number. // She waits. // Then / she says, / "Craig the Cat, / please." //

(254 words)

🔊 音読しよう　　　　　　　　　　　　　　　　　　スピーキング・トレーナー
Practice 1　スラッシュ位置で文を区切って読んでみよう ☐
Practice 2　音声を聞きながら，音声のすぐ後を追って読んでみよう ☐
TRY!　　　　2分30秒以内に本文全体を音読しよう ☐

📖 **Reading**　本文の内容を読んで理解しよう【知識・技能】【思考力・判断力・表現力】　共通テスト

Make the correct choice to complete each sentence or answer each question. (各6点)

1. Wendy is a big fan of ☐ . His name is Craig the Cat.

① a very famous cat　　　　　　② a very famous cat owner

③ a very famous rock star　　　④ a very old rock star

2. Why is Wendy in the lobby of The Dominion Imperial International Hotel? ☐

① To become a rock singer with Craig the Cat.

② To get the latest album from Craig the Cat.

③ To have Craig the Cat sign his autograph on his newest album.

④ To sign her autograph on her latest album.

3. Which of the following is true about the story of Part 1? ☐

① Rosalind is also a big fan of Craig the Cat.

② Rosalind's parents don't know of the rock star.

③ Wendy has never heard of Craig the Cat.

④ Wendy knew that Craig the Cat was staying at The Dominion Imperial International Hotel.

🔍 Vocabulary　　重要表現について理解しよう【知識】　　　　　　　英検® GTEC®

Make the correct choice to complete each sentence. (各3点)

1. The little boy came into the room (　　　　) his teddy bear.

　① dragging　　　② feeding　　　③ handling　　　④ walking

2. The king's people welcomed his return and cheered his (　　　) march.

　① arrogant　　　② humorous　　　③ miserable　　　④ triumphant

3. They are working to make the justice system (　　　) to the needs of victims.

　① addictive　　　② negative　　　③ offensive　　　④ receptive

4. Lucy had to (　　　) the bad story about her from spreading.

　① change　　　② hear　　　③ make　　　④ stop

5. A: This car is no longer in production.

　B: Really? I have never (　　　) of such a thing.

　① heard　　　② help　　　③ made　　　④ spoken

✏️ Production (Write)　　自分の考えを書いて伝えよう【思考力・判断力・表現力】

Write your answer to the following question. (7点)

If you could meet any famous person, who would you meet?

アドバイス　だれに，何のために会いたいかを述べよう。

She looks at me. // "I found him! // Listen!" // She turns the **receiver** / so that I, / too, / can hear. //

A woman is on the other end. // "How did you find out / where Craig the Cat is staying?" / she asks. // "The **leak**. // I need to know / where the leak is." //

"There isn't any. // I'm the only one / with the information. // Please listen. // I want his autograph." //

"Who doesn't?" //

"Help me / get it, / please. // What are my chances?" //

"Poor to **none**." //

"Oh." //

"I'm his manager / and, / my dear, / I'm his mother. // I protect Craig / from two **vantage** points. // Now, / how many other fans know / where he's staying?" //

"None / that I know of." //

"You mean / you didn't sell the information / to the highest **bidder**?" //

"I wouldn't do that." //

"Maybe not, / dear, / but I'm tired of his fans. // Leave him alone! // I'm hanging up." //

Click. //

Wendy **sighs**. // "We'll just have to wait / until he goes into that place / over there / to eat." //

"Haven't you ever heard of room service?" //

"Craig doesn't like room service. // He doesn't like dining rooms, / either. // He's a coffee shop person." //

"How do you know?" //

"I know." //

"How did you know his room number?" //

"I knew." // (195 words)

🔊 **音読しよう**　　　　　　　　　　　　　　　　　　スピーキング・トレーナー

Practice 1　スラッシュ位置で文を区切って読んでみよう ☐
Practice 2　音声を聞きながら，音声のすぐ後を追って読んでみよう ☐
TRY!　　　2分以内に本文全体を音読しよう ☐

📖 **Reading**　本文の内容を読んで理解しよう【知識・技能】【思考力・判断力・表現力】　　　共通テスト

Answer each question. (各6点)

1. What does Craig the Cat's mother mean by "Who doesn't?" ☐

① He doesn't want to sign autographs.

② She doesn't want his son's autograph.

③ She is asking Wendy how many of her friends don't need his autograph.

④ There is no one who doesn't want his autograph.

2. What does Craig's mother think about his fans? ☐

① She thinks his fans are annoying.

② She thinks his fans are attractive.

③ She thinks his fans are too young.

④ She thinks his fans used to be polite but not anymore.

3. What is "that place" that Wendy mentioned in line 19? ☐

① Coffee shop

② Craig the Cat's room

③ Dining room

④ The lobby

🔍 Vocabulary　重要表現について理解しよう【知識】　　　英検® GTEC®

Make the correct choice to complete each sentence. (各3点)

1. Do not turn on the light, in case there is a gas (　　　).

① floating　　　② pouring　　　③ release　　　④ leak

2. When the long speech ended, she let out a (　　) of relief.

① cough　　　② kiss　　　③ sigh　　　④ whistle

3. The sweet voice on the other (　　) reminded him of his grandmother.

① day　　　② end　　　③ foot　　　④ hand

4. My roommate Julia is lazy. I am (　　) hearing her excuses.

① tired　　　② tired of　　　③ tiring of　　　④ tired that

5. Do you see a person who is shouting something (　　) there?

① by　　　② in　　　③ into　　　④ over

✏️ Production (Write)　自分の考えを書いて伝えよう【思考力・判断力・表現力】

Write your answer to the following question. (7点)

Are you a big fan of anybody? Who or what is it?

アドバイス　アーティストや芸能人でもよいし，スポーツ選手でもよい。

We are sitting / in the overstuffed chairs / again. // Wendy is watching and waiting. // I see no human-size cat / in the lobby. // I feel like going to sleep. //

Almost an hour goes by. // Suddenly, / Wendy **pokes** me. // "It's him! // It's him!" //

I look up. // A guy / who seems to be about twenty or twenty-five / is passing by / with a woman / who looks old enough / to be his mother. // He is **lean**. // She is not. // They are dressed **normally**. //

I **whisper** to Wendy. // "*That's* Craig the Cat? // How do you know? // He looks like an **ordinary** guy." //

Wendy doesn't answer. // She stands up / and starts to follow the guy and the woman. // They are heading / for the hotel coffee shop. // I follow all of them. // I see the guy and the woman / sit down. // They are looking at menus. //

Wendy **rushes** up to them, / **clutching** her album. // "May I have your autograph?" / she asks the guy. //

The woman **glares** at Wendy. // "He doesn't give autographs," / she says. // "He's just an ordinary person. // Can't you see / he's just an ordinary person?" //

"*You're Craig the Cat!*" // Wendy says to the guy. //

She says it too loudly. //

"How do you know / I'm Craig the Cat?" / the guy asks. // Also too loudly. //

People in the coffee shop / turn and **stare**. // They repeat, / "Craig the Cat!" //

Suddenly / somebody with a camera appears / and **aims** the camera at Craig. // Wendy **bends** down / and puts her face / in front of Craig's. // It happens so fast, / I can't believe it. // The photographer says, / "Get out of the way, / kid." // (259 words)

🔊 **音読しよう**　　　　　　　　　　　　　　　　　スピーキング・トレーナー

Practice 1　スラッシュ位置で文を区切って読んでみよう ☐
Practice 2　音声を聞きながら，音声のすぐ後を追って読んでみよう ☐
TRY!　　　　2分40秒以内に本文全体を音読しよう ☐

📖 **Reading**　本文の内容を読んで理解しよう【知識・技能】【思考力・判断力・表現力】　　共通テスト

Answer each question. (各6点)

1. What did "A guy" with a woman look like? ☐

   ① He looked like a human-size cat.

   ② He looked like a photographer.

   ③ He looked like an average person.

   ④ He looked like an extraordinary person.

🔊 シャドーイングをすることができる。 　　　　　　　　　　　　　　📖 Part 3を読んで，概要や要点を捉えることができる。
🔍 文脈を理解して適切な語句を用いて英文を完成することができる。
✏️ サインをもらうことについて簡単な語句を用いて考えを表現することができる。

oals

2. What did Wendy do when the guy and the woman started looking at menus? ☐

① She headed for them and tried to take their order.

② She ran to them quickly with the album and talked to them.

③ She sat next to their table and looked at the menu, too.

④ She walked to them slowly with the album and talked to them.

3. What happened when somebody with a camera aimed the camera at Craig? ☐

① Craig ran away from the coffee shop fast.

② People in the coffee shop rushed to Craig.

③ Wendy moved behind Craig to be shot in the same picture.

④ Wendy moved her face in front of Craig's face quickly.

🔍 Vocabulary　重要表現について理解しよう【知識】　　　　　　英検® GTEC®

Make the correct choice to complete each sentence. (各3点)

1. How was your day? ── Well, it was just another (　　) day.
   ① contemporary 　　② extraordinary 　　③ ordinary 　　④ voluntary

2. When the earthquake hit, I was (　　) the counter to keep from falling.
   ① catching 　　② clutching 　　③ getting 　　④ picking

3. The police continued to (　　) at them with suspicion.
   ① aim 　　② glare 　　③ point 　　④ watch

4. Snow White went into the dwarfs' house, (　　) down low.
   ① bending 　　② cooling 　　③ kicking 　　④ touching

5. If you have questions about the class, (　　) the professor's office directly.
   ① come about 　　② get down 　　③ head for 　　④ stay away from

✏️ Production (Write)　自分の考えを書いて伝えよう【思考力・判断力・表現力】

Write your answer to the following question. (7点)

If you meet a celebrity you like, do you rush to him/her to get his/her autograph like Wendy?

アドバイス Yes でも No でも，自分の考え方や性格がどのように影響してその答えになったのかを考えよう。

Craig's mother glares at the photographer. // "**Shoo!**" / she says, / waving her hand. // "Shoo **immediately!**" //

The photographer leaves. // So does Wendy. // She runs back to me. // I am hiding / behind a **fern**. //

Wendy has lost her cool. // "Let's get out of here / before we're kicked out or arrested," / she says. //

We rush toward a door. //

"Wait!" // Someone is **yelling** at us. //

When I hear the word *wait*, / it's a **signal** / for me to move even faster. // But Wendy stops. // "It's *him*!" / she says, / without turning around. //

I turn. // It *is* Craig the Cat. // He's alone. // He rushes up to Wendy. // "How did you know me?" / he asks. // "I didn't tell the media / where I was staying. // And / I certainly didn't give out my room number. // I wasn't wearing my cat **costume**. // And / I was with my mother. // So *how*?" //

Wendy looks at me. // She's trying to decide / if she should answer. // Something in her wants to / and something in her doesn't want to. // She turns back to Craig. // "I'm an expert on you," / she says. // "I know / you like **fancy**, old hotels, / and this is the oldest and the fanciest in town. // I know / your lucky number is twelve, / so I figured / you'd stay on the twelfth floor / in room 1212. // I know / you always wear red **socks** / when you're not performing, / so tonight / I watched **ankles** in the lobby. // And / I knew / you'd be with your manager / —— your mother." // (240 words)

◀)) **音読しよう**   スピーキング・トレーナー
    Practice 1   スラッシュ位置で文を区切って読んでみよう ☐
    Practice 2   音声を聞きながら，音声のすぐ後を追って読んでみよう ☐
    TRY!   2分20秒以内に本文全体を音読しよう ☐

📖 **Reading**   本文の内容を読んで理解しよう【知識・技能】【思考力・判断力・表現力】   共通テスト

Make the correct choice to complete each sentence or answer each question. (各6点)

1. Craig stops Wendy because he wants to know ☐ .

    ① how Wendy reached him

    ② what Wendy has in her hand

    ③ when Wendy came to the hotel

    ④ why Wendy stays here

2. Why does Wendy lose her cool? ⬚

　① Because his mother said "Shoo immediately!" to her.

　② Because she wanted to catch the photographer to get Craig's photo.

　③ Because she was afraid of being kicked out or arrested.

　④ Because she was excited to talk to Craig.

3. Which of the following is **not** true about what Wendy knows about Craig the Cat?

⬚

　① Craig always wears red socks when not performing.

　② Craig likes fancy old hotels.

　③ Craig's lucky number is twelve.

　④ Craig's mother is his photographer.

🔎 Vocabulary　重要表現について理解しよう【知識】　　　英検® GTEC®

Make the correct choice to complete each sentence. (各3点)

1. When a fire breaks out, everyone must evacuate the room (　　　).

　① differently　　　② immediately　　③ repeatedly　　④ slowly

2. The teacher gave us the (　　　) to finish writing and hand in our tests.

　① alarm　　　　② beep　　　　③ call　　　　④ signal

3. He was trying to take deep breaths, knowing he'd lost his (　　　).

　① cool　　　　② mood　　　　③ warmth　　　④ weight

4. It's not good to blame others and (　　　) at them when things go wrong.

　① argue　　　　② fight　　　　③ quarrel　　　④ yell

5. You should wear a jacket when you go to that (　　　) restaurant.

　① casual　　　　② fancy　　　　③ fast-food　　④ overcharging

✍ Production (Write)　自分の考えを書いて伝えよう【思考力・判断力・表現力】

Write your answer to the following question. (7点)

　Have you ever lost your cool? What happened when you lost your cool?

　アドバイス　怒ったときのことを思い出すと考えやすいでしょう。どんな状況だったかを具体的に描写しよう。

"What about the photographer?" //

"I know / you don't want to be photographed / without your cat costume and **makeup**. // In an interview / on October eighth of this year, / you said / it would **wreck** your **feline** image. // So / when I saw the photographer / trying to take your picture, / I put my face / in front of yours." //

"You did that for me?" //

"I'd do it / for any special friend." //

"But you don't know me." //

"Yes, I do. // When I read about someone, / I get to know him. // I don't believe everything / I read, / of course. // I pick out certain parts. // I look for the reality / behind the **unreality**. // I went through seventy-one pages / about Craig the Cat, / in eleven different magazines, / and I ended up thinking of you / as my friend." //

Craig the Cat is staring at Wendy / as if *he's* the fan. // He's in **awe** of *her*! // It's nothing very **earthshaking**. // It's not like there's a crowd **roaring** / or it's a summit meeting of world leaders / or a huge change in the **universe**. // It's just a small, nice moment / in the lobby of The Dominion Imperial International Hotel, / and it will never go away / for Wendy. //

We're back / in the hotel coffee shop. // Four of us are sitting around a table, / eating. // Craig's mother is **beaming benevolently** / like a **contented** mother cat / **presiding** over her **brood**, / which now includes Wendy and me / in addition to Craig. // After we finish eating, / Wendy hands her record album to Craig. // "Now / may I have your autograph?" / she asks. // (253 words)

🔊 **音読しよう**

スピーキング・トレーナー

Practice 1　スラッシュ位置で文を区切って読んでみよう ☐
Practice 2　音声を聞きながら，音声のすぐ後を追って読んでみよう ☐
TRY!　　　2分30秒以内に本文全体を音読しよう ☐

📖 **Reading**　本文の内容を読んで理解しよう【知識・技能】【思考力・判断力・表現力】　　共通テスト

Make the correct choice to complete each sentence or answer each question. (各6点)

1. Why did Wendy put her face in front of Craig's when a photographer aimed his camera at him? ☐
   ① To be photographed with him.
   ② To disturb the photographer trying to take Craig's photo.
   ③ To pick up his cat costume on the floor.
   ④ To see if he was wearing red socks.

2. After hearing Wendy's words, Craig thought that ☐.

① he would forgive her

② she was a person who believed whatever she heard

③ she was different from other fans

④ she was rude

3. How did Craig's mother feel toward Wendy and Rosalind in the last paragraph?

☐

① She was angry as they joined the table.

② She was anxious because other fans may come and join them.

③ She was fond of them and sees them as his friends.

④ She was suspicious of their intention.

🔍 Vocabulary　重要表現について理解しよう【知識】　　　　　　英検◎ GTEC◎

Make the correct choice to complete each sentence. (各3点)

1. The people are in (　　　) of the sacred mountain and see it as god.

① awe　　　　② case　　　　③ spite　　　　④ terms

2. The typhoon hit this area last year and (　　　) hundreds of houses.

① affected　　② fell　　　　③ tore　　　　④ wrecked

3. When he scored in the final, the supporters (　　　) and whistled for joy.

① cried　　　② discouraged　③ roared　　　④ whispered

4. After solving a difficult problem, there was a very happy and (　　　) smile on both of their faces.

① artificial　② compromise　③ contented　④ depressed

5. The company has been (　　　) over by him for over 30 years.

① elected　　② predicted　　③ presided　　④ run

✎ Production (Write)　自分の考えを書いて伝えよう【思考力・判断力・表現力】

Write your answer to the following question. (7点)

If you were Craig the Cat, what would you say to Wendy?

アドバイス　ウェンディがどんなファンであるかを知ったあと，クレイグは彼女に対してどう思ったか，想像してみよう。

When Paul was quite young, / his family had one of the first telephones / in their **neighborhood**. //

I remember well the **wooden** case / **fastened** to the wall / on the stair **landing**. // The receiver hung / on the side of the box. // I even remember the number / — 105. // I was too little / to reach the telephone, / but used to listen **eagerly** / when my mother talked to it. // Once / she **lifted** me up / to speak to my father, / who was away / on business. // Magic! //

Then / I discovered / that **somewhere** inside that wonderful device / lived an amazing person / — her name was "Information Please" / and there was nothing / she did not know. //

My mother could ask her / for anybody's number; / when our clock ran down, / Information Please immediately supplied the correct time. //

My first personal experience / with this woman-in-the-receiver / came one day / while my mother was visiting a neighbor. // **Amusing** myself / with a **hammer**, / I hit my finger. // The pain was terrible, / but there didn't seem to be much use crying / because there was no one home / to hear me. // I walked around the house / **sucking** my finger, / finally arriving at the landing. // The telephone! // Quickly / I ran for the **footstool** / and took it / to the landing. // Climbing up, / I took the receiver / and held it to my ear. // "Information Please," / I said into the **mouthpiece** / just above my head. // (226 words)

 音読しよう 　　　　　　　　　　　　　　　　　　　　　　　スピーキング・トレーナー
Practice 1　スラッシュ位置で文を区切って読んでみよう ☐
Practice 2　音声を聞きながら，音声のすぐ後を追って読んでみよう ☐
TRY!　　　　2分20秒以内に本文全体を音読しよう ☐

📖 **Reading**　本文の内容を読んで理解しよう【知識・技能】【思考力・判断力・表現力】　　共通テスト

Make the correct choice to complete each sentence or answer each question. (各6点)

1. Which of the following is **not** true? ☐

　① Paul was able to reach the receiver of telephone with no help.

　② Paul's family had one of the first telephones in their neighborhood.

　③ Telephone was like magic to Paul.

　④ The telephone number of Paul's family was 105.

2. Paul thought the person living inside the device was amazing because ☐ .

① she had an unusual name "Information Please"

② she was able to do a magic show

③ she was so small to live in such a small device

④ there was nothing she did not know

3. What was Paul's first personal experience with "Information Please"? ☐

① It was when he hit his finger while playing with a hammer.

② It was when he needed the correct time as his clock was down.

③ It was when he tried to talk to his father who was away from home.

④ It was when he wanted to know somebody's telephone number.

🔍 Vocabulary　　重要表現について理解しよう【知識】　　　　　英検® GTEC®

Make the correct choice to complete each sentence. (各3点)

1. Wherever we went, my son asked (　　　　) for the names of things he saw for the first time.

　① eagerly　　　　② generally　　　　③ hopefully　　　　④ merely

2. When a rainy day kept us indoors, we (　　　　) ourselves with chatting or playing video games.

　① amused　　　　② enjoyed　　　　③ played　　　　④ teased

3. Only female mosquitoes (　　　) blood in order to produce eggs.

　① chew　　　　② draw　　　　③ eliminate　　　　④ suck

4. There is no (　　　) expecting to catch any fish at this time of the day.

　① choice　　　　② mean　　　　③ use　　　　④ way

5. He (　　　) the new watch, which he just got from his sons as a gift, to his wrist.

　① attached　　　　② fastened　　　　③ rolled　　　　④ wrapped

✏️ Production (Write)　　自分の考えを書いて伝えよう【思考力・判断力・表現力】

Write your answer to the following question. (7点)

　Do you have your own cellphone? What did you think when you first got your own cellphone?

　アドバイス　　はじめて手に入れたときのことを思い出してみよう。

A click or two, / and a small, clear voice / spoke into my ear. // "Information." //

"I hurt my fingerrrrr ——" / I cried into the phone. // The tears began running down, / now that I had an audience. //

"Isn't your mother home?" / came the question. //

"Nobody's home / but me," / I said. //

"Are you bleeding?" //

"No," / I **replied**. // "I hit it / with the hammer / and it hurts." //

"Can you open your **icebox**?" / she asked. // I said / I could. //

"Then / break off a little piece of ice / and hold it / on your finger. // That will stop the hurt. // Be careful / when you use the ice pick," / she warned. // "And don't cry. // You'll be all right." //

After that, / I called Information Please / for everything. // I asked for help / with my **geography** / and she told me / where Philadelphia was, / and the Orinoco / —— the river / I was going to explore / when I grew up. // She helped me / with my **arithmetic**, / and she told me / that a pet **chipmunk** / —— I had caught him / in the park / just the day before / —— would eat fruit and nuts. //

And / there was the time / that our pet **canary** died. // I called Information Please / and told her the sad story. // She listened, / and then said the usual things / grown-ups say / to **soothe** a child. // But I did not feel better: / why should birds sing so beautifully / and bring joy / to whole families, / only to end as a **heap** of **feathers** / feet up, / on the bottom of a cage? //

She must have sensed my deep concern, / for she said quietly, / "Paul, / always remember / that there are other worlds / to sing in." //

Somehow / I felt better. // (273 words)

🔊 音読しよう

スピーキング・トレーナー

Practice 1　スラッシュ位置で文を区切って読んでみよう ☐
Practice 2　音声を聞きながら，音声のすぐ後を追って読んでみよう ☐
TRY!　　　　2分40秒以内に本文全体を音読しよう ☐

📖 **Reading**　本文の内容を読んで理解しよう【知識・技能】【思考力・判断力・表現力】　共通テスト

Answer each question. (各6点)

1.　Who is "an audience" in line 3? ☐

　① Paul himself

　② Paul's neighbors

　③ Paul's mother

　④ The woman-in-the-receiver

2. Which of the following is **not** mentioned as a memory with "Information Please"?

① She helped Paul with arithmetic.

② She taught him what chipmunks eat.

③ She taught him where Philadelphia and the Orinoco were.

④ She taught him why canaries sing so beautifully.

3. Which of the following is the most suitable title for Part 2?

① Children Are Frequently Involved in Accidents

② Children Are Not Supposed to be Left Alone

③ Losing a Pet Is Always Depressing

④ How "Information Please" Helped Paul

🔍 Vocabulary　重要表現について理解しよう【知識】　　　　　　　　英検® GTEC®

Make the correct choice to complete each sentence. (各3点)

1. The (　　　) of this area is so complicated that even local people get lost.
   ① biography　　　② calligraphy　　　③ geography　　　④ philosophy

2. Animals such as dogs are believed to (　　　) your pain; it is called Animal Therapy.
   ① bite　　　　　② catch　　　　　③ defeat　　　　　④ soothe

3. Now (　　　) I know the truth, I'm sure I'll feel better.
   ① for　　　　　② on　　　　　③ that　　　　　④ then

4. After the hurricane passed, nothing but a (　　　) of ruins remained in the town.
   ① crowd　　　　② group　　　　③ heap　　　　　④ pack

5. His music was powerful and yet (　　　) touching.
   ① anytime　　　② anyway　　　③ somehow　　　④ somewhere

✎ Production (Write)　自分の考えを書いて伝えよう【思考力・判断力・表現力】

Write your answer to the following question. (7点)

Do you have any memory of spending time alone in your childhood?

アドバイス　何歳のときか，どう感じたかの記憶を描写しよう。

Another day / I was at the telephone. // "Information," / said the now **familiar** voice. //

"How do you spell fix?" / I asked. //

"Fix something? // F-I-X." //

At that **instant** / my sister, / trying to **scare** me, / jumped off the stairs at me. // I fell off the footstool, / pulling the receiver / out of the box. // We were both **terrified** / — Information Please was no longer there, / and I was not at all sure / that I hadn't hurt her / when I pulled the receiver out. //

Minutes later / there was a man at the door. // "I'm a telephone **repairman**. // I was working down the street / and the **operator** said / there might be some trouble / at this number." // He reached for the receiver / in my hand. // "What happened?" //

I told him. //

"Well, / we can fix that / in a minute or two." // He opened the telephone box, / did some repair work, / and then spoke into the phone. // "Hi, / this is Pete. // Everything's under control / at 105. // The kid's sister scared him / and he pulled the **cord** / out of the box." //

He hung up, / smiled, / gave me a **pat** on the head / and walked out of the door. //

All this took place / in a small town / in the Pacific Northwest. // Then, / when I was nine years old, / we moved / across the country to Boston / — and I missed Information Please / very much. // She belonged in that old wooden box back home, / and I somehow never thought of trying the tall, **skinny** new phone / that sat on a small table / in the hall. // (252 words)

◀))) 音読しよう　　　　　　　　　　　　　　　　　　　スピーキング・トレーナー

Practice 1　スラッシュ位置で文を区切って読んでみよう ☐
Practice 2　音声を聞きながら，音声のすぐ後を追って読んでみよう ☐
TRY!　　　2分30秒以内に本文全体を音読しよう ☐

📖 **Reading**　本文の内容を読んで理解しよう【知識・技能】【思考力・判断力・表現力】　　共通テスト

Make the correct choice to complete each sentence or answer each question. (各6点)

1.　Why was Paul terrified when he pulled the receiver out out of the box? ☐

① Because he hadn't finished the spelling question.

② Because he thought it might hurt the lady on the other end.

③ Because he thought their parents would get mad at him.

④ Because it might hurt his sister.

2. The telephone repairman came to Paul's house so quickly because ⬚ .

   ① any trouble of telephone was automatically informed to repairpersons

   ② he heard the noise when working down the street

   ③ his sister went out and called for a help

   ④ the operator sent him to Paul's house

3. After Paul' family moved to Boston, he didn't try to call Information Please as ⬚ .

   ① he forgot about her while living a new life

   ② he had grown up enough not to ask childish questions

   ③ he didn't think that she belonged in the skinny new phone

   ④ his parents prohibited him from making long distance calls

🔎 **Vocabulary**　　重要表現について理解しよう【知識】　　英検Ⓡ GTECⓇ

Make the correct choice to complete each sentence. (各3点)

1. The (　　　) faces at the high school reunion brought Charles back to his teenage days.

   ① familiar　　　② muscular　　　③ peculiar　　　④ similar

2. In (　　　) he caught the bug and smashed it on the floor.

   ① a hurry　　　② advance　　　③ an instant　　　④ fact

3. He was (　　　) of being scolded by his mother.

   ① identified　　② occupied　　③ simplify　　④ terrified

4. My older brother (　　　) off his horse and broke his ankle.

   ① fell　　　　　② put　　　　　③ took　　　　　④ turned

5. Listening to favorite music helps her get her emotions under (　　　).

   ① construction　② control　　③ investigation　④ pressure

✍ **Production (Write)**　　自分の考えを書いて伝えよう【思考力・判断力・表現力】

Write your answer to the following question. (7点)

　Have you ever broken something in your house?　How did you feel then?

　アドバイス　壊したことがない場合でも，補足的な情報を加えよう。

Yet, / as I grew into my **teens**, / the memories of those childhood conversations / never really left me; / often in moments of **doubt** and worry / I would **recall** the **serene** sense of **security** / I had / when I knew / that I could call Information Please / and get the right answer. // I **appreciated** now / how patient, understanding and kind she was / to have wasted her time / on a little boy. //

A few years later, / on my way west to college, / my plane landed in Seattle. // I had about half an hour / before my plane left, / and I spent 15 minutes or so / on the phone / with my sister, / who had a happy **marriage** there now. // Then, / really without thinking / what I was doing, / I dialed my hometown operator / and said, / "Information Please." //

Miraculously, / I heard again the small, clear voice / I knew so well: / "Information." //

I hadn't planned this, / but I heard myself saying, / "Could you tell me, / please, / how to spell the word 'fix'?" //

There was a long **pause**. // Then / came the softly spoken answer. // "I guess," / said Information Please, / "that your finger must be all right / by now." //

I laughed. // "So / it's really still you. // I wonder / if you have any idea / how much you meant to me / during all that time …" //

"I wonder," / she replied, / "if you know / how much you meant to me? // I never had any children, / and I used to look forward to your calls. // **Silly**, / wasn't it?" //

(241 words)

🔊 **音読しよう**

スピーキング・トレーナー

Practice 1　スラッシュ位置で文を区切って読んでみよう ☐
Practice 2　音声を聞きながら，音声のすぐ後を追って読んでみよう ☐
TRY!　　　2分30秒以内に本文全体を音読しよう ☐

📖 **Reading**　本文の内容を読んで理解しよう【知識・技能】【思考力・判断力・表現力】　　共通テスト

Answer each question. (各6点)

1. On what occasion did Paul often recall "Information Please"? ☐
   ① When he didn't know the answer to his homework.
   ② When he didn't know what his pet eats.
   ③ When he needed to know the correct time.
   ④ When he was in moments of doubt and worry.

2. Why did Paul fly to Seattle when he grew into his teens? ☐

　① Because he needed to meet his sister who lived there.

　② Because he wanted to talk to "Information Please."

　③ Because he went to a collage located in the west.

　④ Because his plane landed there with some mechanical trouble.

3. Why was there a long pause when Paul asked the lady how to spell 'fix'? ☐

　① Because she didn't know how to spell it.

　② Because it took her some time to remember her experience with Paul.

　③ Because she was surprised to know that the caller didn't know how to spell it.

　④ Because there was a line trouble between them.

🔍 Vocabulary　重要表現について理解しよう【知識】　　　　　　　　　英検® GTEC®

Make the correct choice to complete each sentence. (各3点)

1. She wanted to send him a letter but couldn't (　　　) his address.
　① consider　　　② memorize　　　③ notice　　　④ recall

2. The King stood there remaining (　　　) in dignity.
　① funny　　　② loud　　　③ serene　　　④ weird

3. (　　　), she survived the car accident.
　① Absolutely　　② Miraculously　　③ Obviously　　④ Relatively

4. Don't blame him for (　　　) money on gaming. It is his money.
　① checking　　　② leaving　　　③ reducing　　　④ wasting

5. Give me an hour (　　　). I will prepare dinner.
　① by now　　　② by then　　　③ once more　　　④ or so

✎ Production (Write)　自分の考えを書いて伝えよう【思考力・判断力・表現力】

Write your answer to the following question. (7点)

　If you were Paul, would you call "Information Please" when you were at the airport in Seattle?

　アドバイス　ポールの気持ちを想像してみよう。

....

....

It didn't seem silly, / but I didn't say so. // Instead / I told her / how often I had thought of her / over the years, / and I asked / if I could call her again / when I came back / to visit my sister / after the first **semester** was over. //

"Please do. // Just ask for Sally." //

"Goodbye, / Sally." // It sounded strange / for Information Please to have a name. // "If I run into any chipmunks, / I'll tell them / to eat fruit and nuts." //

"Do that," / she said. // "And / I expect one / of these days / you'll visit the Orinoco. // Well, / goodbye." //

Just three months later / I was back again / at the Seattle airport. // A different voice answered, / "Information," / and I asked for Sally. //

"Are you a friend?" //

"Yes," / I said. // "An old friend." //

"Then / I'm sorry / to have to tell you. // Sally had only been working part-time / in the last few years / because she was ill. // She died five weeks ago." // But before I could hang up, / she said, / "Wait a minute. // Did you say / your name was Willard?" //

"Yes." //

"Well, / Sally left a message / for you. // She wrote it down." //

"What was it?" / I asked, / almost knowing in advance / what it would be. //

"Here it is, / I'll read it / —— 'Tell him / I still say / there are other worlds / to sing in. // He'll know / what I mean.' " //

I thanked her / and hung up. // I did know / what Sally meant. // (235 words)

🔊 音読しよう   スピーキング・トレーナー
Practice 1   スラッシュ位置で文を区切って読んでみよう □
Practice 2   音声を聞きながら，音声のすぐ後を追って読んでみよう □
TRY!   2分20秒以内に本文全体を音読しよう □

📖 **Reading**   本文の内容を読んで理解しよう【知識・技能】【思考力・判断力・表現力】   共通テスト

Make the correct choice to complete each sentence or answer each question. (各6点)

1. Why did "Sally" sound strange to Paul? ⬚

① Because he didn't expect her to give him her real name.

② Because he was used to calling her "Information Please."

③ Because it was the same name as his sister's.

④ Because "Sally" was a strange name.

2. Three months later at the Seattle airport, Paul called "Information" as ☐ .

① he had an extra time before leaving

② he had no one to talk with as his sister was away

③ he had something he wanted to solve

④ he wanted to talk to Sally

3. What did Sally imply by "other worlds to sing in"? ☐

① The world full of canaries.

② The world living things go after their death.

③ The world where people who live there like to sing together.

④ The world where people don't need "Information."

🔍 **Vocabulary & Grammar**　　重要表現や文法事項について理解しよう【知識】　　　　　英検® GTEC®

Make the correct choice to complete each sentence. (各3点)

1. We will have some exchange students during the spring (　　).

① break　　　　　② semester　　　　③ span　　　　④ table

2. I am (　　) to have kept you waiting.

① able　　　　　② fine　　　　　③ sorry　　　　④ sure

3. My mother (　　) lunch for me when she left home.

① ate　　　　　② fed　　　　　③ gave　　　　④ left

4. You must pay for the trip (　　) advance.

① at　　　　　② by　　　　　③ in　　　　④ on

5. He (　　) want to see the movie.

① do　　　　　② does　　　　③ really　　　④ then

✐ **Production (Write)**　　自分の考えを書いて伝えよう【思考力・判断力・表現力】

Write your answer to the following question. (7点)

What is your happiest childhood memory?

アドバイス　自分が幸せだと思うことならどんなことでも構わないので，思い出して描写してみよう。

WPM・得点一覧表

●スピーキング・トレーナーを使って，各レッスンの本文を流暢に音読できるようにしましょう。下の計算式を使って，1分あたりに音読できた語数（words per minute）を算出してみましょう。

【本文の総語数】÷【音読にかかった時間(秒)】×60
= ☐ wpm

Lesson		WPM	得点
1	Part 1	/ wpm	/ 40
	Part 2	/ wpm	/ 40
	Part 3	/ wpm	/ 40
	Part 4	/ wpm	/ 40
	AP	/ wpm	/ 40
	流暢さの目安 100 wpm		/ 200

Lesson		WPM	得点
2	Part 1	/ wpm	/ 40
	Part 2	/ wpm	/ 40
	Part 3	/ wpm	/ 40
	Part 4	/ wpm	/ 40
	AP	/ wpm	/ 40
	流暢さの目安 100 wpm		/ 200

Lesson		WPM	得点
3	Part 1	/ wpm	/ 40
	Part 2	/ wpm	/ 40
	Part 3	/ wpm	/ 40
	Part 4	/ wpm	/ 40
	AP	/ wpm	/ 40
	流暢さの目安 100 wpm		/ 200

Lesson		WPM	得点
4	Part 1	/ wpm	/ 40
	Part 2	/ wpm	/ 40
	Part 3	/ wpm	/ 40
	Part 4	/ wpm	/ 40
	AP	/ wpm	/ 40
	流暢さの目安 100 wpm		/ 200

Lesson		WPM	得点
5	Part 1	/ wpm	/ 40
	Part 2	/ wpm	/ 40
	Part 3	/ wpm	/ 40
	Part 4	/ wpm	/ 40
	AP	/ wpm	/ 40
	流暢さの目安 100 wpm		/ 200

Lesson		WPM	得点
6	Part 1	/ wpm	/ 40
	Part 2	/ wpm	/ 40
	Part 3	/ wpm	/ 40
	Part 4	/ wpm	/ 40
	AP	/ wpm	/ 40
	流暢さの目安 100 wpm		/ 200

Lesson		WPM	得点
7	Part 1	/ wpm	/ 40
	Part 2	/ wpm	/ 40
	Part 3	/ wpm	/ 40
	Part 4	/ wpm	/ 40
	AP	/ wpm	/ 40
	流暢さの目安 100 wpm		/ 200

Lesson		WPM	得点
8	Part 1	/ wpm	/ 40
	Part 2	/ wpm	/ 40
	Part 3	/ wpm	/ 40
	Part 4	/ wpm	/ 40
	AP	/ wpm	/ 40
	流暢さの目安 100 wpm		/ 200

Lesson		WPM	得点
9	Part 1	/ wpm	/ 40
	Part 2	/ wpm	/ 40
	Part 3	/ wpm	/ 40
	Part 4	/ wpm	/ 40
	AP	/ wpm	/ 40
	流暢さの目安 100 wpm		/ 200

Optional		WPM	得点
1	Part 1	/ wpm	/ 40
	Part 2	/ wpm	/ 40
	Part 3	/ wpm	/ 40
	Part 4	/ wpm	/ 40
	Part 5	/ wpm	/ 40
	流暢さの目安 100 wpm		/ 200

Optional		WPM	得点
2	Part 1	/ wpm	/ 40
	Part 2	/ wpm	/ 40
	Part 3	/ wpm	/ 40
	Part 4	/ wpm	/ 40
	Part 5	/ wpm	/ 40
	流暢さの目安 100 wpm		/ 200